WORKING TOGETHER IN CHILD PROTECTION

This book is dedicated to Ciaran, Catherine, Timothy Patrick and Roisin. Also to all child protection practitioners, who give of their skill, effort and hope in ways that frequently go unrecognised.

Working Together in Child Protection

An exploration of the multi-disciplinary task and system

Michael Murphy

arena

Published by
Arena
Ashgate Publishing Limited
Gower House
Croft Road
Aldershot
Hants GU11 3HR
England

Ashgate Publishing Company
Old Post Road
Brookfield
Vermont 05036
USA

British Library Cataloguing in Publication Data
Murphy, Michael
    Working Together in Child Protection:
    Exploration of the Multi-disciplinary Task and System
    I. Title
    362.7680941
ISBN 1 85742 197 3 (hardback)
ISBN 1 85742 198 1 (paperback)

Library of Congress Cataloging-in-Publication Data
Murphy, Michael, 1955–
    Working together in child protection: an exploration
    of the multi-disciplinary task and system / Michael Murphy
        p. cm.
    Includes bibliographical references and index.
    ISBN 1–85742–197–3 (cloth): £30.00 ($55.95 US: est.)
    – ISBN 1–85742–198–1 (pbk): ($25.00 US: est.)
    1. Social work with children – Great Britain. 2. Abused
    Children – Services for – Great Britain. 3. Child abuse
    – Prevention.
    I. Title
    HV751.A6M87 1994   94–20449
    362.7'0941 – dc20   CIP

Phototypeset in 10 point Palatino by Intype, London and printed in Great Britain by Hartnolls Ltd, Bodmin

Contents

List of figures

Preface

This book was partly inspired by government advice and guidance about multi-disciplinary child protection work, which always seemed to presume too much. This book does not presume too much – it explores, it explains and it attempts to be helpful and relevant to practice.

To illustrate particular points within the text, use is made of a number of practice scenarios. These scenarios are relevant examples of practice that have been disguised to protect the identity of the participants concerned.

Finally, because the majority of basic-grade practitioners in the child protection system are women, practitioners are referred to as 'she' rather than 'he' within the text.

Acknowledgements

I would like to acknowledge the contribution of my friends and colleagues in Bolton ACPC, the training pool, the Social Services training section and all the practitioners in the Bolton child protection system, who have helped me to understand the complexities of multi-disciplinary child protection work. I would like to thank Dr Neil Thompson for his constructive criticism of the text. Most of all, my thanks to Anne Paterson for her consistent encouragement and positive attitude.

Glossary of terms

ACPC	The Area Child Protection Committee. The multi-agency coordinating committee for child protection work.
BEd	Bachelor of Education. A four-year teaching qualification.
breached	The re-calling to court of an offender who has breached a community court order (*Probation Service*).
case	A family, a child, a unit of work (*Social Services*).
case conference	A multi-disciplinary meeting, held under child protection procedures, to share information and decide on future action.
caseload	A health visitor or field social worker's workload.
Cert Ed	Certificate of Education. A three-year teaching qualification.
Child Assessment Order	A court order (Children Act 1989) that allows access to children to assess them.
child protection plan	A plan made at a case conference for multi-agency action with regard to a child on the register.
client	A consumer of the social work service.
core group	The group of multi-disciplinary practitioners charged with the job of carrying out the child protection plan.
CPS	The Crown Prosecution Service. The agency responsible for guiding prosecutions for child abuse through the criminal legal process.
CQSW	Certificate of Qualification in Social Work. The former qualification in social work (2–4 years).

CSS	Certificate in Social Service. The former residential social work qualification (3 years).
de-registered	The removal, by a review conference, of a child's name from the Child Protection Register.
DES	Department for Education and Science.
designated teacher	The member of staff within the school who has responsibility for child protection matters.
DipSW	Diploma in Social Work. The combined qualification for field and residential social work.
DMS	Diploma in Management Studies.
DoH	Department of Health.
duty officer	The social worker responsible for incoming child protection referrals (often part of an intake team).
Emergency Protection Order (EPO)	A legal order (replacing the Place of Safety Order) that permits the removal of a child to a safe environment.
failure to thrive	An exaggerated form of physical or emotional neglect, in which very young children fail to grow and develop.
FHSA	Family Health Services Authority.
fieldwork (*Social Services*)	Social work in the community (not in a residential or daycare setting).
fieldwork (*Youth Service*)	Direct work with young people in the Youth Service.
first parenting	A special form of preventative health visitor support for first-time parents.
FRCP	Fellow of the Royal College of Physicians.
guardian ad litem	A specialist independent social worker representing the interests of the child in the care process.
intake team	A specialist social work team which takes all referrals of new work. Often responsible for child protection investigations.
Koerner	The elaborate, occasionally oppressive, system of quantifying and recording the use of school nurse and health visitor time.
LEA	Local Education Authority.
level 2 or 3	Newly-qualified social workers are appointed on level 2 pay scale and grade, but are allowed to progress to a level 3 grade after a certain amount of experience has been gained. In theory this means that the most difficult cases will be reserved for the level 3 social worker.

LMS	Local Management of Schools (the devolution of power to school governing bodies).
MBA	Master of Business Administration. A higher degree in management, increasingly popular in helping agencies.
memorandum interview	A joint interview in child sexual abuse undertaken by the social worker and the Police.
MRCGP	Member of the Royal College of General Practitioners.
NAI	This stands for non-accidental injury or a case of child physical abuse (now an old term but still in regular use).
non-abusing parent	The parent (frequently in child sexual abuse) who is unaware that the abuse has occurred.
NVQ	National Vocational Qualifications. A series of work-based qualifications of increasing importance in the helping agencies.
office tie	The shared item of apparel that male social workers use when going to court.
opting out	The ability of schools to 'opt out' of the local authority system or sphere of influence.
organised abuse	The systematic (sexual) abuse of children by a group of often unrelated adults.
PAIN	Parents Against Injustice.
parental participation	The attendance and inclusion of the parents of the abused child in the multi-disciplinary child protection meetings.
perpetrator	A perpetrator of child sexual abuse.
PGCE	Post-Graduate Certificate of Education. A one-year teaching qualification for graduates.
planning meeting	An informal multi-disciplinary meeting called to discuss concerns about a particular child before a referral is made.
professional abuse	The abuse of a child by the practitioner responsible for her care.
referral	A new piece of (child protection) work received by the field social work team.
registered	This means that a child's name has been placed, by a case conference, on the Child Protection Register.
RGN	Registered General Nurse. The current general nursing qualification.
ritualistic abuse	Organised abuse with satanic overtones.

SATs	Specialist Assessment Teams. Specially established multi-disciplinary teams for working with difficult child sexual abuse cases.
Schedule 1 offence	A serious offence perpetrated against a child.
SRN	State Registered Nurse. A former general nursing qualification.
SSI	The Social Services Inspectorate (a regulatory social work body).
statutory case	A case in which a legal order has been made for the care and protection of a child.
TSP	Training Support Programme. An annual grant to Social Services Departments to fund specific areas of training including child protection work.
unallocated	This indicates that, although the Social Services Department are aware of the situation, a social worker has not been allocated to the case. In terms of a registered child, this would mean that the child had no keyworker (usually due to a shortage of resources).

Introduction

Welcome to this book about multi-disciplinary child protection work! It attempts to be theoretically challenging and practically useful. It is one book among several that are published every year on the subject of child protection, but it does hold one fundamental difference. It is not about child protection *per se* but about the exploration of child protection work as a multi-disciplinary task or effort. This book does not claim, as some have done in the past, to bequeath an ultimate expertise, to be the last book on child protection that you will ever have to read! This book is about facilitating our practice by the better understanding of our system. This does not just include the narrow understanding of our own role, but the wider understanding of the roles of other practitioner groups.

Child protection work in Britain sometimes seems to be in danger of becoming seen as the domain of the expert. In child protection terms no one expert, or single area of expertise, will ever be enough. To pretend that this might be so would be to exaggerate the importance of any one practitioner at the expense of the wider multi-disciplinary group. We all have our own area of expertise within our own practice domain. These different areas of expertise should complement each other, forming the basis of effective cooperative action. However, we are often ignorant of the expertise of our colleagues and are not good at explaining our own area of expertise to others.

If we compare the child protection process to a game, the decades since the 1960s have seen an increase in knowledge or expertise about the rules of the game, and an increase in the technical understanding of what needs to be done within it. But this rise in expertise has ignored one crucial element in child protection work – it is essentially a team task. Although individual ability, training and expertise are important, the child protection task is not one that is amenable to processing through the sole expertise of one individual practitioner or practitioner group.

Therefore, what good is the most suitable therapeutic facility if the right families are not referred to it? What use is the most advanced form of direct work with the individual abused child if she is accommodated in an unsuitable, unsympathetic residential or foster home? How effective is the most sensitive handling of a disclosure of child sexual abuse if the child goes on to be bullied within the court system? Child protection work is a complementary, collective process that needs the positive contribution of all concerned.

Child protection work is difficult. It can be personally and professionally stressful. It can, and frequently does, create considerable anxiety in the practitioner and the agency, who feel obliged to 'get it right' all the time. This work will not patronise the reader by suggesting that there are easy or 'right' answers to the problems that child abuse raises. However, the work will not attempt to 'awfulise' child protection work either. It can be an area of work full of job satisfaction, stimulation and even enjoyment. It will also continue to be a crucial element in how any society cares for one of its most numerous, most vulnerable groups of citizens.

This work seeks to explore the multi-disciplinary context of child protection work. It examines difficult areas of practice and suggests possible helpful developments. Without denying the inherent difficulty of the child protection task, it seeks to test the hypothesis that the development of good multi-disciplinary teamwork is the most crucial element in improving child protection practice.

It might be said that the work is not radical enough – that the real answer to multi-disciplinary child protection work is either to remove child abuse by a revolutionary change in society, or to remove the need for multi-disciplinary work by a similar change within the system. The former is not within the purview of this book: major change, though sometimes welcome, often fails to solve the original problem and creates new tensions in its wake. The latter seems more plausible. Butler-Sloss (1988), following the Cleveland controversy, suggested the formation of SATs – small, specialist teams – that would combine all the different practitioner skills in one place. The logical sequel to this proposal is to create a new child protection agency that combines all the different skills and functions under one roof. However, the development of such an agency seems unlikely; a survey undertaken in 1991, for a different piece of work, suggested that only two areas in England and Wales possessed teams that evenly remotely resembled a SAT (Murphy 1995). The development of a specialist agency could be financially and politically difficult, would probably still fail to deal with all child protection referrals and would lack the wide knowledge and practitioner base that is necessary for good child protection work. This book therefore, though not afraid to suggest change, does so largely within the current multi-disciplinary framework.

The book is set out in the following way:

Part I sets the context for the rest of the work.

Chapter 1 looks at the definitional problems around multi-disciplinary child protection work, examines the historical development of such work in the USA and England and Wales, and suggests some parameters for understanding the tensions in the child protection task.

Chapter 2 examines what the multi-disciplinary child protection task is, how it is undertaken and how it is coordinated.

Chapter 3 explores the difficulty of multi-disciplinary child protection work. Its primary hypothesis is that this difficulty is not the fault of the individual practitioner, but is due to the structural difficulties involved in inter-agency collaboration. The chapter goes on to examine, with appropriate examples, what these structural issues are.

Part II takes, in turn, a major agency or group of agencies, examining in detail their role, perspective and pressures in working in the child protection arena. This section includes examples of difficult areas of practice and provides useful general information on the structure of these agencies.

Chapter 4 is concerned with the differing roles, perspectives and problems of the members of the Social Services Department.

Chapter 5 is concerned with the roles, perspectives and problems of the different members of the Health Service.

Chapter 6 is concerned with the different roles and perspectives of the Education and Youth Service.

Chapter 7 deals with the differing roles of those agencies and practitioners who are involved in the legal system.

Chapter 8 is concerned with the voluntary organisations that have played such an important role in the development of the child protection service.

Part III explores the individual and organisational paths to positive multi-disciplinary practice.

Chapter 9 looks away from the agency context of multi-disciplinary work towards the impact of the individual on that inter-agency work and the impact of the work on the individual.

Chapter 10 begins to draw some conclusions about the achievement of positive multi-disciplinary work, examining the differing responsibilities for making inter-agency collaboration work. It also examines the different contexts of child protection work, drawing conclusions about how to improve collaboration at different points within the child protection process.

Chapter 11 draws the book together by reformulating the major themes of the previous ten chapters and offering a summary of the major issues to be addressed in multi-disciplinary child protection practice.

The whole work aims to be informative for the practitioner, the manager and the trainee. It is based both in theory and practice, but attempts, most of all, to be useful to those currently involved in child protection work. Throughout the text use is made of practice scenarios – these are suitably disguised examples of current practice, used to illustrate particular points in the book. Please use the book in the way that best suits your interest or learning need – either by reading it as a whole or by 'dipping in' to chapters that have particular relevance for you.

This work begins with a challenge to the reader – we all harbour a deep ignorance not just of the child protection system *per se*, but of the role and perspective of the other practitioner groups within that system.

If you agree with this statement, you may choose to read on to do something about it. If you disagree with this statement, you may choose to read on to test it out!

Part I

The multi-disciplinary context

1 What is multi-disciplinary child protection work?

This book will not attempt to patronise practitioners who work within the child protection system by attempting to suggest, as do some inquiries and government publications, that multi-disciplinary child protection work is obvious or easy. Part of the task of this book is to begin to uncover the layers of difficulty that exist within the system, suggesting ways of addressing such issues in a positive fashion.

The definition

Before beginning an examination of the history of the multi-disciplinary child protection system, it would be helpful to suggest a definition of, or at least to define the parameters of, such a system. But even such an initial step is hedged round with difficulty:

> it might be thought that practitioners from various agencies and professional perspectives should share a common understanding about the conditions that constitute child abuse ... it would also be helpful if such professional definitions should be derived from standards accepted by the community at large. But both these pre-requisites are far from simple. (Hallett and Birchall 1992, p.101)

To say that such a system is socially constructed or defined would seem to be an obvious but essential initial proposal:

> Child abuse is a phenomenon which is dependent for its existence on the perceptions of those involved in the interaction and those external audiences who must first identify and then intervene. (Christopherson 1989, p.75)

Thus, there is little within the child protection arena that is given. Rather, inclusion within this arena is dependent upon decisions about what child abuse is and what should be included, with what priority, in the subject area:

> child abuse is not a naturalistic category – nothing is 'naturally' child abuse. It is only child abuse if it has been proscribed in a given society and if the control agencies act in such a way as to enforce that proscription. (Parton 1985, p.148)

What is clear is that such a societal perspective, such a societal proscription, will differ between societies or communities and will also change over time. Gordon (1989), in her study of child abuse in Massachusetts, makes it clear that there were differences in how both social workers and families defined what was appropriate childcare practice. She also points out that societal perceptions of appropriate childcare practice change over time, so that legitimate parental control in one generation can come to be seen as abuse in the next.

Childhood

As far as child protection itself is concerned, the difficulties of achieving a permanent and satisfying definition are considerable. Even the concept of what childhood is and when it starts and finishes is subject to a great deal of variation and debate, both in legal and social terms. Aries (1962) has claimed that in medieval times the concept of childhood was not distinct from adulthood. Aries's thesis has been challenged on several grounds, most notably on the grounds that different societies can hold different, but still appropriate, conceptualisations of childhood. 'What cannot be sustained, however, is Aries's key claim that past societies lacked the concept of childhood. They merely possessed a different conception' (Archard 1993, p.23).

The western world still harbours many different or inconsistent ways of defining childhood. For example, when does the foetus become a person in its own right? At what age does the child develop the ability in law to speak and be believed in her own right? When does childhood end for a young person with severe learning disability? These have all been recent debates around the nature of the definition of childhood in western society.

Child protection

The concept of child protection has grown out of a previous concept of 'child abuse'. The term 'child abuse' implied a harmful interaction between carer and cared for, with responsibility for that interaction attributed to the carer. The coming of the concept of child protection has brought several extra dimensions to the equation, not least a more positive responsibility on the part of the practitioner and protection system for the early prevention of that abusive interaction.

The multi-disciplinary child protection system

When looking at the wider subject area of the multi-disciplinary or inter-agency system, definitional difficulties remain. Who should be included in or excluded from the system; should the system be made up of all the independent parts of the child welfare system or just those parts that frequently interact around child abuse?

Hallett and Birchall (1992) found that to try to define the multi-disciplinary system in terms of its activity was also fraught with difficulty, discovering that there were many types of separate activity, priority and perspective that might have to be included within the definition.

Little help is offered by the various official government publications on child protection. It seems that it is presumed that what is and what is not multi-disciplinary child protection work is somehow self-evident.

The definition that I would like to suggest for the purpose of this work is:

> The coming together, by more than one agency or practitioner group, to act in a collaborative way to prevent the occurrence or re-occurrence of abuse with regard to a particular child, or children in general, and to offer such therapeutic help as those children, and their families, require.

This definition presumes that more than one agency or practitioner group must be involved, that an element of positive collaboration is essential (rather than one agency acting on behalf of others, or two agencies competing against each other). This collaboration can be aimed at prevention, protection or more long-term therapeutic needs.

It is important, at this stage, to emphasise what is *not* within our definition of good multi-disciplinary work – that is, the taking control, either over the work itself or over how the work is defined, by one agency or one agency's perspective. If this does occur, then multi-disciplinary work becomes merely a question of you seeing the problem from my perspective and then thinking and behaving more like me. This is not collaboration or cooperation, it is colonialism – or, more accurately, colonisation – of one agency or practitioner by another.

Practice scenario 1.1

In the core group meeting the field social worker and the teacher were in the middle of an argument. The social worker was worried about the case and wanted to take a course of action that had not been agreed by the multi-disciplinary group. The teacher was polite but insistent, although she too was worried. From her recent discussions with the child concerned, she felt that what the social worker was suggesting would not be an appropriate course of action to take. The social worker claimed the right to independent action; the teacher acknowledged this right, but questioned the use of it within the core group. The social worker fell silent, lost in thought, eventually agreeing that unilateral action was not appropriate and that the core group should agree any new course of action.

Within this interaction the social worker had come to realise that other agencies and practitioners had the right to hold separate perspectives and opinions, and the right for them to be influential in the child protection plan.

Child protection perspectives

No society will enjoy a single perspective on child protection. The intricacies and ambivalences that surround state intervention into family life do not allow a single perspective to be utilised: 'Consensus is illusory once the complexities are probed ... The debates [about perspectives] are significant because of the serious dilemmas that arise in policy, and because different perspectives point to different policy consequences' (Fox Harding 1991, p.3). A perspective is a series of perceptions, beliefs and ways of understanding a problem, which are intertwined with the making of policy. A series of three perspectives have been developed for another piece of work (Murphy 1995) – the family welfare, the child protection and the children's rights perspectives. These perspectives compete to inform state thinking and then state action.

The family welfare perspective has as its core belief (in all but the most exceptional circumstances) that the needs and interests of the child and the parent will be the same (or at least similar enough to ensure the child's wellbeing). This perspective seeks a minimal level of state intrusion into family life and is wary of giving too much intrusive power to the child protection system.

The child protection perspective acts as the antithesis of the family welfare perspective; it holds as its key tenet that the needs of parents and the needs of children are not necessarily conterminous and are, in fact, frequently in conflict. This perspective believes in the positive nature of state intervention, and is willing to allow intrusive intervention into family life to prevent child abuse.

These two perspectives are the main tools that the state uses to inform child protection policy. In historical terms, the two can be seen to be constantly in competition – when one is in the ascendancy the other, though still present, will have a reduced sphere of influence (see Figure 1.1). In effect, the discussion about policy will revolve around a system that either actively seeks out abuse or only reacts to the most extreme examples of that abuse, when they become obvious in the public arena.

The above, powerful perspectives rely on an adult-centred definition of abuse. The third, least powerful perspective attempts to give back to the child – the object of that abuse – some control over the whole process. The children's rights perspective believes that children can be both nurtured and oppressed within the family, but that allowing them more control over their own treatment and destiny (rather than ignoring them or rescuing them in an intrusive fashion) provides the key to the struggle against child abuse.

Of the three perspectives, it is the family welfare perspective that enjoys the most influence, with the child protection perspective acting as its counterpoint. The children's rights perspective is relatively weak, reflecting the general status of children in our society (see Figure 1.1).

The family welfare and child protection perspectives exist at either end of a continuum of positions (see Figure 1.2) with historical periods, child protection systems, agencies and individual practitioners located somewhere on that continuum. Since the two perspectives are in competition, the holding of opposite perspectives by different agencies and practitioners can strongly affect collaborative work.

In total, the definition of multi-disciplinary child protection work is dependent upon society's understanding of several related themes, including childhood, reasonable parenting, abuse and appropriate multi-disciplinary action. The choice of societal policy will depend on the interplay and relative power of the perspectives that society holds on the subject of child protection.

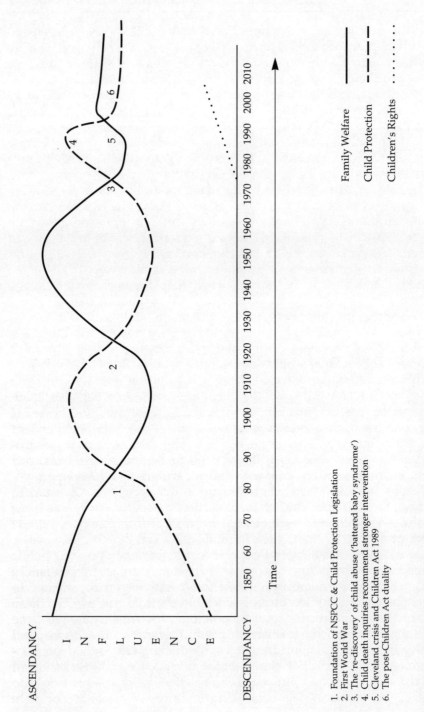

ASCENDANCY

I
N
F
L
U
E
N
C
E

DESCENDANCY

Time

1850 60 70 80 90 1900 1910 1920 1930 1940 1950 1960 1970 1980 1990 2000 2010

1. Foundation of NSPCC & Child Protection Legislation
2. First World War
3. The 're-discovery' of child abuse ('battered baby syndrome')
4. Child death inquiries recommend stronger intervention
5. Cleveland crisis and Children Act 1989
6. The post-Children Act duality

————— Family Welfare

– – – – – Child Protection

·········· Children's Rights

Figure 1.1 The influence of action perspectives

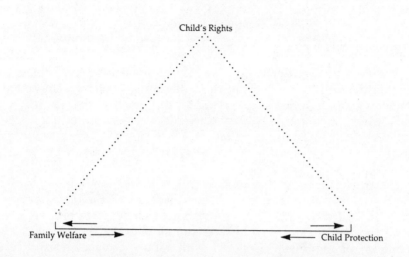

Figure 1.2   The continuum of child protection perspectives

The history of multi-disciplinary child protection work

No child protection system is created in a vacuum. The historical development of each system will be individual and will be dependent upon the interplay between the different societal perspectives on protection, the relationship between the system's constituent parts, and the unfolding 'ownership' of the problem within the given society.

This book does not seek to give an analysis of the global development of multi-disciplinary child protection work, but uses as an example the child protection system in England and Wales, offering pertinent comparisons with other systems around the world.

The nineteenth century, in Britain and the USA, saw a growing public concern about the effects of urbanisation and industrialisation on family life. A series of voluntary organisations were set up to attempt to highlight and help particularly vulnerable parts of that family. These organisations included those who aimed to protect animals (the RSPCA), women (the Society for the Protection of Women and Children) and finally children (the voluntary child welfare organisations and the NSPCC – the National Society for the Prevention of Cruelty to Children). All of these organisations recognised the need to protect the vulnerable by some kind of intrusive voluntary or state intervention: 'Educated Scots and Englishmen were growing increasingly sensitive to the problem of parental cruelty and were now prepared to countenance a cautious child protection effort' (Behlmer 1982, p.77).

In Britain this cautious effort was largely driven by the SPCCs, who created the will to move away from the family welfare perspective in terms of social policy, and provided the inspectorate to deal with individual cases of cruelty. A partnership was established that left the voluntary organisations, especially the NSPCC, with the specific child protection task, whilst the statutory agencies maintained the residual, generalist role.

The period between the First World War and the beginning of the 1960s was one of quietness or latency in terms of the development of child protection work. Child protection itself was largely out of the public gaze. Gordon (1989) links this quiet period with the diminished influence of feminism: 'Concern with family violence usually grew when feminism was strong and ebbed when feminism was weak' (p.4). This hypothesis might also help to explain the differential development of child protection systems between different countries, linking this development to the strength of their feminist movements.

This period of latency marked a strong period of ascendancy for the family welfare perspective, emphasising as it did the positive nature of the family: 'It is almost as if it was assumed that a conflict of interests between child, parents and the state had disappeared and the nineteenth-century problems of cruelty and neglect had been virtually abolished' (Parton 1985, p.45).

This period drew to a close, in the USA, in the late 1950s and early 1960s, when the Kempes and their paediatric associates in Colorado (Kempe et al. 1962) instituted a series of research projects which led to the establishment of the 'battered baby' syndrome. This work was transposed into the British context through the NSPCC's Denver House project, which instituted a treatment service in London using the model formulated by the Kempes in the USA.

The two systems, even though influenced at that stage by similar information and research, developed two very different approaches to multi-disciplinary working. In the USA, a domination of the multi-disciplinary field by paediatricians was combined with an early involvement of the legal system. Thus, by the end of the 1960s, most of the individual states had introduced special child protection legislation, often including the compulsory reporting of child abuse by all relevant practitioners and agencies. In Britain, although the involvement of paediatricians was crucial to the multi-disciplinary system (see Chapter 5), it was the NSPCC who pioneered many of the early developments in child abuse work. These early developments did not produce major legislative changes; indeed the developments to the system were ushered in through government circular. The USA's legal obligation to report abuse was never replicated in the British system; in fact, this lack of legal compulsion and a strong emphasis on voluntary cooperation was to be a key component in the development of the British multi-disciplinary system.

The NSPCC planned to extend the work of the Denver House project by establishing a series of teams in large conurbations that would have built-in access to multi-disciplinary consultation, and would try to include some elements of multi-disciplinary working within themselves. According to Pickett and Maton (1979), the Manchester unit, which opened in 1973, was to include: 'a team of six qualified social workers ... a Health Visitor ... a family centre staffed by five qualified Nursery Nurses. There is also a team of consultants in Paediatrics, Psychiatry, Gynaecology and Obstetrics and the Law ... A team of volunteers is also used' (p.117). The unit was to attempt to promote multi-disciplinary working by drawing in to itself both the case conference system and the expertise of concerned agencies (this model has many similarities to the confidential doctor centres in Belgium and the Netherlands).

However, this system could only be relevant to those few areas with an NSPCC unit and with a referral rate of abuse that could be processed by a single team. The rise of a more general awareness of abuse increased the level of referral to such an extent that larger organisational systems were needed that could not be dependent on the resources of a single voluntary organisation.

The development of the multi-disciplinary system

The 're-discovery' of physical abuse in Britain occurred at an inopportune moment for its statutory social work agencies. The Social Services Act 1970 had subsumed the specialist Children's Departments into the larger, generic Social Services Departments, which had then been reorganised in 1974. In the 1960s it might have seemed obvious that the Children's Departments could take on a facilitating role in the new service, but in the 1970s who could shoulder this burden? In the USA it had clearly been the medical profession who had taken that crucial facilitating role.

Despite their state of unreadiness, the death of Maria Colwell in 1973 was to plunge the new Social Services Departments into the centre of the new, multi-disciplinary system. It is difficult to under-estimate the effect of Maria's death and the subsequent inquiry. Parton (1985) claims that they gave rise to a moral panic about the family in general and child abuse in particular, which catapulted child abuse from its position of low importance to a position at centre stage: 'The case of Maria Colwell proved crucial in establishing the issue as a major social problem and in introducing fundamental changes in policy and practice' (p.65).

Maria Colwell died from physical abuse in January 1973, when she was seven years old. In the years which preceded her death, workers from each of the key agencies – Social Services, Education, Health, Police, Housing and the NSPCC – had all been involved with Maria and her family. During the course of the inquiry their interactions were weighed, investigated and commented upon. The inquiry was to lead to a series of new perceptions about how agencies were to work together in future.

Three consequent themes were to dominate the development of the multi-disciplinary system in England and Wales.

Communication

One of the central themes in the Colwell Inquiry was that it was the failures in multi-disciplinary communication and cooperation that were to blame for 'at risk' children not being identified and afforded protection. The report referred on numerous occasions to failures in communication: 'the fatal failure to pool the total knowledge of Maria's background, recent history and physical and mental condition' (DHSS 1974, p.53).

Repeated inquiries into child deaths were to emphasise the crucial role of multi-disciplinary communication in the prevention and recognition of child abuse. Lack of coordination and communication was frequently cited as a key contributor to children's deaths through physical abuse: 'Every report reveals problems in some aspect of communication between individuals and agencies, which is not surprising in view of the sheer number involved in each case' (DHSS 1983, p.48).

In 1988 the Cleveland Report (Butler-Sloss 1988) was the first major report to deal specifically with the phenomenon of child sexual abuse (awareness of which had been growing in Britain during the 1980s). It was to change the emphasis of the understanding of multi-disciplinary communication. Instead of poor communication leading to children being more at risk of physical abuse, lack of communication was now seen as largely to blame for the over-identification of child sexual abuse, rather than the under-identification of physical abuse. The Cleveland crisis and subsequent inquiry were to witness the differing parts of the multi-disciplinary system failing to communicate and engaging in bitter conflict over control over the new subject area. This seriously affected the service that children received: 'It is unacceptable that the disagreements and failure of communication of adults should be allowed to obscure the needs of children ... The children had unhappy experiences which should not be allowed to happen again' (Butler-Sloss 1988, p.244).

Responsibility

The Colwell Report drew back from laying the blame for Maria's death on the individual practitioner: 'we think it quite impossible, and indeed unfair, to lay the direct blame ... upon any individual or indeed upon any small group of individuals' (DHSS 1974, p.86). Instead the report laid the blame on the shoulders of the agencies concerned, and eventually the government:

> it seems to us that certain local authorities and agencies in Maria's case cannot escape censure because they must accept responsibility for the errors and omissions of their workers; because they are responsible for their supervision, and because at all levels they failed to devise efficient and, so far as is humanly possible, fail-safe systems. (DHSS 1974, p.87)

Although the report repeatedly emphasised the need for the whole multi-disciplinary system to take responsibility for child abuse work, it envisaged two special areas of responsibility.

The first was to suggest that the Social Services Department rather than the NSPCC should have responsibility for coordinating the system. The report was highly critical of the duplication between the two agencies and suggested that the NSPCC concentrate on their experimental role: 'We simply comment that if the NSPCC is considering a long-term shift of emphasis it might be to the benefit of children at risk both by the avoidance of duplication and by the development of specialised treatment and research in the NSPCC' (DHSS 1974, p.71).

The second was to indicate clearly the need for governmental intervention and ultimate responsibility: 'Because that system is the product of society it is upon society as a whole that the ultimate blame must rest ... It is not enough for the state as representing society to assume responsibility for those such as Maria. It must also provide the means to do so' (DHSS 1974, p.86).

The Colwell Inquiry plainly suggests that one area of governmental responsibility was to be the provision of a child protection system. The report was duly followed by the government issuing a series of guidances in the form of circulars to the multi-disciplinary system. Throughout the late 1970s and early 1980s, child death inquiries were followed by similar government circulars:

> These inquiries have played a crucial role in the development of public and political concern, and have provided the impetus for stimulating administrative and management procedures for identifying and handling cases of child abuse. Their impact in helping to usher in changes in policy and practice in this area have probably been more significant than if substantive pieces of legislation had been put on the statute book as happened in numerous other countries. (Parton 1985, p.101)

The intervention of the state became more overt with the publication of the first *Working Together* consultation document (DHSS 1986), which was closely followed by *Working Together* Marks 1 and 2 (DHSS 1988; DoH 1991c). These publications aimed to make the differential responsibilities within the system clear and attempted to marry these with the other major governmental contribution to the system, which was the substantive piece of legislative change, the Children Act 1989.

The issue of responsibility within the system has reflected the same duality since 1974. As envisaged by the Colwell Report (DHSS 1974), responsibility for facilitating the system was given to the Social Services Department rather than the NSPCC or Health Authority. But this facilitation was to be achieved through the wider multi-disciplinary umbrella of the local Area Child Protection Committees (ACPCs). At the same time as the Social Services Department kept this crucial coordinating role, other key agencies would maintain their right to independence of decision and action. The tension between this duality of collective and individual responsibility is one of the key facets of multi-disciplinary systems.

The most serious threat to this duality came with the publishing of the Cleveland Report (Butler-Sloss 1988), which recommended the setting up of multi-disciplinary assessment teams (SATs) which were to bring all practitioners within one unified body and thus obviate the problem of inter-agency working. This recommendation was referred to (but not endorsed) in *Working Together* (DHSS 1988). However, by 1992 only two areas in England and Wales contained teams that resembled a 'SAT'; the rest maintained the traditional multi-disciplinary network (Murphy 1995).

The system

The Colwell Report repeatedly emphasised the need for a suitable system that would enable practitioners to communicate and interact in a more effective way: 'The overall impression created by Maria's sad history is that while individuals made mistakes it was the "system", using the word in the widest sense, which failed her' (DHSS 1974, p.86). It would be up to the government to suggest the outline and legal boundaries of such a system, and up to the multi-disciplinary group of agencies to make that system work, with a key coordinating role going to the Social Services Department.

The search for the foolproof system began shortly after the publication of the Colwell Report. The guidance for this system was contained in the same series of circulars that established responsibility within the multi-disciplinary field. The hypothesis behind this development was that such a system would go a long way to making up for individual errors, lack of training and difficulties in the inter-agency system.

Although the advice of the government was to become more prescriptive in terms of the system (for example, the *Working Together* documents defined the categories for registration and the criteria for registration and de-registration), the actual working of the different local systems showed a remarkably stubborn local variation (Bingley Miller, Fisher and Sinclair 1993).

Despite the considerable development of child protection systems, inquiries into child deaths still showed that lack of expertise and poor multi-disciplinary communication and performance heightened the possibility of child death or injury. What the search for a foolproof system failed to address was the need for improved training and professional performance within the system.

The 1990s have seen the same three themes – communication, responsibility and systematisation – being developed in the British multi-disciplinary system. The Children Act 1989 introduced a new era where the family welfare perspective gradually regained the ascendancy over the child protection perspective. This meant that the need for communication between agencies, although still an important theme, was matched by the insistence on the need to communicate with parents.

In the area of responsibility, the government intervened with legislation and guidance that continually re-shaped the multi-disciplinary system. After the Children Act 1989, decisions that were to be made about forcible intervention into families' lives (concerned with abuse) were to be made far more under the supervision of the legal system. One of the problems associated with this growth in power of the legal system was that it presumed that better judgments would consequently be made. (Chapter 7 will consider this matter in greater detail.)

Conclusion

We have seen that a child protection system will be influenced and formulated by the conflicting definitions of and perspectives on child-care and child abuse that a society holds. This system will also be influenced by the shape of the existing professional network in general childcare and by the roles which agencies take or are given within the process. Any new child protection system will be built around that existing network and will be influenced by how society and childcare agencies react to the new protection task.

The crucial dilemma around which the system will be built is that of the child's independent right not to be abused and the parent's right not to be interfered with by agents of the state.

As Fox Harding (1991) points out:

> Concerns about the child care agents of the state doing too much, too coercively, and about them doing too little, too ineffectually, resulted in a wish for legislation and policy to attempt to proceed in two directions at once – both towards better protection of the child and better protection of the parent. (p.230)

This is the key debate for all child protection systems: how well will they be able to hold these mutually antagonistic demands at the forefront of their work? How well will they be able to intervene strongly to prevent serious abuse and to act in a non-interventionist way towards those families where the threat of serious abuse is a false one? Or, as Fox Harding asks, can a balance be struck between these two poles of behaviour, or is constant conflict between the two inevitable? Chapter 2 examines how these problems are addressed in the working of the child protection system in England and Wales.

2 How one system works

This chapter explores what actually happens within the work of one child protection system. This includes: who is in the system; how the system is organised and funded, and how the system processes the cases of child protection that are fed into it.

But is there a need for such a chapter? Surely the practitioners and families within a given system will already know how it works? Unfortunately, although it is presumed that the practitioner, the child and the family will have an understanding of what occurs within a given child protection system, this assumption is frequently incorrect. There is a strong tendency within child protection activity for participants to understand fully only that part of the system in which they are directly involved, the rest of the system remaining largely a mystery to them. This might prove of concern when the incremental nature of child protection work is considered. One agency's action directly affects the subsequent actions of other agencies; the reasons why a particular path was chosen might have crucial significance in later therapeutic work: 'Professionals of all agencies need to recognise how their own task and action influence the task of fellow professionals and how in turn their own task is affected by the process in other parts of the professional network' (Furniss 1991, p.xvii).

All systems will not be the same; there will be differences between child protection systems in how they perceive the problem and in how they operate. Sale and Davies (1990) have collected information from many European child protection systems that indicates a very large divergence in organisation and practice between one system and another. For example, whilst the child protection system in Greece is still combatting the large-scale denial that child abuse is a problem, the Scandinavian systems have achieved an environment where all physical assault on children is illegal (even though in many Scandinavian families violence is still customary, according to Sariola and Uutela (1993)).

For the purpose of this chapter, the British system will be used as an appropriate example of how a child protection system operates. However, even within Britain there is much diversity. The Scottish system operates under its own legal system, whilst in the six counties of Northern Ireland the joint Health and Social Services boards, which collectively manage many Health and Social Services practitioners, make up a very different organisational context for child protection work.

In England and Wales, despite prescriptive government guidance (DoH 1991c), there is still substantial divergence between and within local systems (Bingley Miller, Fisher and Sinclair 1993). This leeway or discretion is used to decide what (or who) should be included within the system and what is the best course of action to be taken with regard to a particular case. It is possible, for example, for exactly the same abusive situation to lead to registration in one district, whilst in a neighbouring district registration might not be considered appropriate. One multi-disciplinary system that adopted a more child protection perspective (see Chapter 1) might recommend registration, whilst another, adopting a more family welfare perspective, judges this to be inadvisable. This means that what is discussed below is taken either from the organisation and behaviour of one specific system or, alternatively, is a description of an 'ideal-type' system, which is an amalgam of 'typical' characteristics from many British child protection systems.

The Area Child Protection Committee

Following the death of Maria Colwell in 1973 the British government realised that there was a need for a single body to try to coordinate child protection work at a local level. Since that time all child protection systems in England and Wales have been coordinated by bodies originally named Area Review Committees (ARCs) and currently called Area Child Protection Committees (ACPCs). Their functions include the coordination and monitoring of the child protection effort and the training of staff within their multi-disciplinary system. They will issue child protection procedures, help resolve inter-agency disputes and review individual cases when something goes wrong. This compulsory provision of a coordinating committee is substantially different to the system in the USA, where coordinating committees, where they do exist, are the result of local, voluntary effort (Skaff 1988).

Evans and Miller (1993) have commented on the increasing role of the ACPC within the system, as a facilitator of government policy:

'ACPCs are now used as major avenues through which the government implements its guidelines. Their expanded role also covers monitoring of practice, training and service development' (p.7). In order to be able to complete these functions effectively the British ACPC has need of power and resources. In actuality it possesses neither in any great supply; there is an assumption that the traditional, voluntary cooperation between member agencies will be sufficient to allow the committee to do its work.

Membership

The full ACPC will encompass a relatively large group of between 20 and 50 persons. The majority of this membership will be drawn from the four big organisations – Police, Education, Social Services and Health. Health can be particularly well represented because of the need for all sections of health provision (for example, paediatrics, community trust, hospital trust, the purchaser, the FHSA, GPs, child and adult psychiatry, and so on) to be represented separately. At the same time, other smaller organisations that have important childcare roles will have a representative sitting on the committee. The Probation Service, the Magistrate's Court, the NSPCC and other voluntary social work organisations are all likely to be represented. Finally, the ACPC has the right to co-opt on to the committee any other practitioner or organisation that it thinks can help it in its child protection task. The make-up of the British committee is very similar to that of the coordinating committees in the USA, with the notable exception of representation from consumer groups (Skaff 1988). This lack of consumer representation is seen by Evans and Miller (1993) as one of the weaknesses of the system.

The committee will primarily have a professional or managerial focus rather than a political one: elected members, MPs or leaders of specifically political groups seldom hold membership. This is in sharp contrast to some other European countries (most notably Denmark) where elected representatives are central to the process. In Britain, this lack of elected representatives constitutes an attempt to make the ACPC into a politically 'neutral' body.

The key roles of chairperson and deputy chairperson of the committee will usually be allocated to senior Social and Health Service staff.

Structure

Because of the size and multiplicity of ACPC tasks, specific functions are frequently delegated to smaller subsidiary committees, whose membership is drawn from the larger ACPC (see Figure 2.1). The four larger agencies (Health, Education, Police and Social Services) will be well represented on the smaller committees, as they are in the parent body.

One style of organisation which is often utilised is that of a small executive committee, meeting regularly to deal with day-to-day business, which reports back to the larger committee, which meets much less frequently. The ACPC will also delegate specific tasks to sub-committees, which again report their recommendations and actions back to the wider committee. Typically these sub-committees might include:

- A procedures or guidelines sub-committee which would be responsible for the production, updating and distribution of the local child protection procedures. This sub-committee's workload can be particularly heavy at times when government produces major changes in legislation or guidance.
- A training sub-committee responsible for organising multi-disciplinary training events. This committee might attempt to provide a minimum level of training for new practitioners in an ACPC area.
- A review sub-committee set up to review cases of child death, injury or other serious abuse, which might also monitor standards of practice within the system generally.

The ACPC has the ability, where necessary, to set up other standing sub-committees or *ad hoc* working groups with a specific task to perform. Giller, Gormley and Williams (1992) found that one sub-committee in authority A in their study had been set up by the ACPC to: 'review and quality-assure the management of registered children's cases and ratify the de-registration decisions of case conferences' (Appendix D).

It is sometimes the case that the same personnel represent their agency on the ACPC, the executive and the various sub-committees. Although this can lead to better working relationships and sense of 'teamwork', as this group learns to function well together, it can leave a sense that these key members have a monopoly of power within the system. This can leave the representatives of the smaller organisations in a relatively powerless position. Skaff (1988) comments on the surprisingly democratic culture of US committees; this is not replicated in British ACPCs, where different member organisations wield different levels of influence and power. Evans and Miller (1993) have argued that, in England and Wales, there is a two-tiered hierarchy of power, with the Police and Social Services occupying the most powerful tier and other organisations operating in the second tier. Although agreeing that the system has become tiered in a hierarchical fashion, it seems that Evans and Miller's analysis fails to fully recognise some aspects of

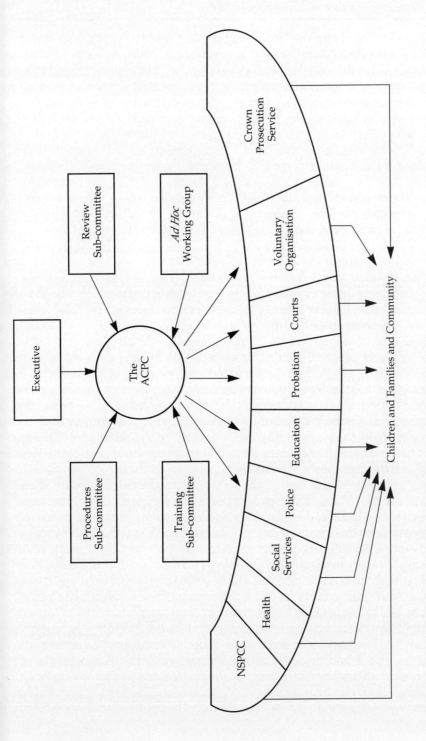

Figure 2.1 The typical Area Child Protection Committee

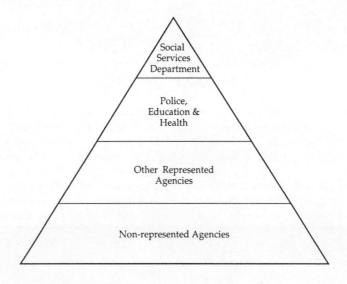

Figure 2.2   Hierarchy and power in ACPCs

that hierarchy. It would seem more accurate to suggest a four-tiered system (see Figure 2.2), with Social Services occupying the most influential sphere, followed by the Police, Education and Health in the second. The third tier is occupied by other represented agencies (for example, the Probation Service, the NSPCC and the courts) and the fourth by those organisations not given any representation at all. This might include small voluntary organisations, consumer groups and less involved local authority departments.

It should be remembered, however, that power within the system still depends on the ability to persuade other organisations to pursue a particular course of action. The Social Services Department has no statutory power within the ACPC: 'the agency [Social Services] primarily responsible for child protection does not have the authority to command the cooperation of other agencies or to coordinate their activities' (Utting 1993, p.5).

Accountability, power and resources

British ACPCs are not resourced or funded from central government. They rely instead on voluntary contributions from local agencies to resource their functions: 'Agencies should allocate funds to the ACPC in accordance with agreed arrangements at the beginning of each financial year so that the ACPC has an annual budget' (DoH 1991c, p.7). On occasions this advice to contribute is not followed and the burden of supporting the ACPC is unevenly shared.

Practice scenario 2.1

For some time the Coltown ACPC had struggled to establish a budget to fund its operations. Eventually Social Services, Health, Police and even some of the smaller organisations had made their contributions. The only exception was the Education Service, which steadfastly resisted all attempts to make it contribute, much to the annoyance of its own representatives. This non-contribution led to some inter-agency frustration at what was seen as a 'subsidisation' of one agency by others. Whenever monetary matters arose on the agenda, the ACPC found itself discussing Education's non-contribution rather than concentrating on the best use of existing resources.

The result of this under-resourcing is that the ACPC frequently has to rely on the goodwill of local agencies for even the most basic of its organisational needs (such as its stationery or its secretarial support).

The members of the committee are required to have a certain power or standing within their own organisation:

> Their appointees should have sufficient authority to allow them to speak on their agencies' behalf and to make decisions to an agreed level without referral to the appointees' agencies. The level of decision-making delegated to appointees needs to be considerable to enable ACPCs to operate effectively. (DoH 1991c, p.6)

Although this senior status is useful in terms of policy, ACPCs can sometimes seem far removed from the reality of the basic-grade practitioner. In fact, it is not uncommon for relatively new child protection staff to be unaware of the role (or even existence) of the ACPC.

These committee members are in fact not accountable to the ACPC, but are accountable to the organisations that they represent. So, in essence, the ACPC is a voluntary gathering, with no direct power, except in that it can persuade constituent organisations to do what it recommends. In this the ACPC closely mirrors each multi-disciplinary conference or core group, where control lies not within the group but back in member organisations.

This lack of resources, allied to accountability outside the committee, leaves the ACPC in a potentially weak position in its role as a coordinator. Effectively, unless it can achieve consensus between its constituent parts, progress and change can be very difficult to achieve.

However, a well-coordinated ACPC can exert a strong 'moral' and 'political' influence on its constituent parts that member organisations find difficult to resist.

Practice scenario 2.2

'Familymakers' was a voluntary organisation working in Bigtown that had always had an independent attitude to child protection work. The organisation was part-funded by the local authority. This independence was tolerated until a problem arose with a particular child protection case. The ACPC and its sub-committees went into action. Training for the whole staff group was offered. The chair of the procedures sub-committee went to the agency bearing several copies of the new procedures. The chair of the whole ACPC organised a meeting where it was insisted that the organisation fall into line; if not a complaint would be issued to its funding bodies. Thus, by a process of persuasion, 'moral' and 'political' pressure, the voluntary organisation was persuaded to follow the ACPC's lead.

The process

After discussing the macro-organisational structure of the child protection system, it is appropriate to examine the micro system, or what actually happens within the system, in terms of the individual practitioner and child (for whom the ACPC is likely to be a very distant and mysterious body).

Many different types of abuse are recognised by the child protection system in England and Wales: these include physical, sexual and emotional abuse; neglect; failure to thrive; ritualistic or organised abuse, and institutional and professional abuse. Although there are substantial differences between these types of abuse, the way that they are processed through the child protection system is often very similar. It is appropriate to look for those commonalities in the process. What are the core elements that are involved in the child protection process? What demands do they make on the staff who make up the multi-disciplinary system? How is their day-to-day work coordinated and run?

The stages of the process

There exists a series of stages through which a child protection case may pass (Figure 2.3), but it is important to remember that at each

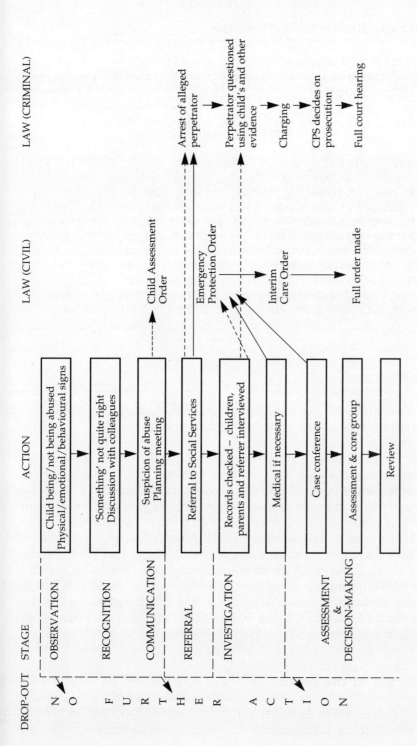

Figure 2.3 The stages of the child protection process

stage it is possible for the child and family to 'drop out' of the system rather than proceed to the next stage. Many cases do not pass beyond the investigation stage; very few will reach the stage of legal proceedings. This 'drop-out' rate can best be explained in terms of the 'significant harm' criteria in the Children Act 1989. At each stage it is asked whether the child has suffered, or is likely to suffer, significant harm. If the answer is yes, the child proceeds to the next stage. If no, the child 'drops out' of the system. At the same time, if the child is considered to be in extreme danger, at any stage of the process, an Emergency Protection Order may be requested (usually by Social Services from a Magistrate's Court) that can remove the child for a short period of time to a safer environment (see Legal proceedings, pages 38–9).

The series of stages within the system is as follows:

- Observation and recognition
- Referral
- Investigation
- Conference
- Assessment and review (see Figure 2.3).

Each stage is outlined below.

Observation and recognition

Many children pass through the care of practitioners in the British child protection system every day. Of these, several hundred will exhibit signs or behaviour indicative of what could potentially be abuse – bruising, inappropriate sexualised behaviour, exaggerated sadness, and so on. If all these children were referred through the child protection system, the system would very quickly collapse through overload. It is the job of the practitioners in the protection system to sift the signs that have been caused by 'normal' childhood occurrences from those that are likely to have been caused by intra-familial child abuse. These practitioners have the crucial task of putting into the system what the system has to process. This task is not easy: if they refer too frequently the system will collapse and their judgment will be questioned; if too infrequently then children who are being abused will not be brought to the notice of the protective system.

Most child protection procedures under-estimate the difficulty of this stage of recognition: 'any person who has knowledge of, or a suspicion that a child is suffering significant harm, or is at risk of significant harm, should refer their concern to one or more of the agencies with statutory duties and/or power to investigate or intervene' (DoH 1991c, p.27). Procedures presume that recognition is a straightforward affair, but, in practice, it often is not.

Dingwall, Eekelaar and Murray (1983) argue that there are certain belief systems that prevent practitioners from recognising the signs of abuse. The most influential of these they call the 'rule of optimism'. This leads to a belief on the part of an individual practitioner that child abuse would not happen in their class, patient list or caseload. This belief can significantly reduce the ability of the practitioner to identify abuse. It is possible for a whole agency, practitioner group or even society to indulge in the 'rule of optimism'. Papatheophilou (1990) claims that Greek society would prefer to deny the existence of child abuse altogether, rather than admit that it can be an integral part of family life in Greece. However, in practice, the 'rule of optimism' can be gradually eroded by the feeling that something is 'not quite right' with regard to a particular child or family. At some time a Rubicon will be crossed when the practitioner will begin to suspect abuse; further evidence may then lead to subsequent referral. Often it is difficult for the practitioner to judge if that Rubicon has actually been passed, in which case it is advisable for the staff member to get help both from within her own agency and from the outside system. Within the British system, the pre-referral planning meeting offers a multi-disciplinary forum, before a referral proper is made. On occasion, practitioners who have had their awareness of child abuse raised by reading or by training can express fears that they will employ a 'rule of pessimism', and see abuse in every child that they work with.

Practice scenario 2.3

Alison was a headteacher from Castlepark primary school. Her school had never made a referral of child abuse. She had attended the training course on child sexual abuse for information and more knowledge, but did not feel that it would really affect families in her school (because 'they were not really like that'). The course shook Alison's confidence in the impossibility of child abuse occurring in Castlepark. Two months later she made her school's first referral through the procedures.

Although the course worried the headteacher, and increased markedly her referral rate, that referral, that worry and that increased awareness of child protection matters were entirely functional and appropriate.

Referral

The referral is another stage in the child protection process that is often not explained adequately in procedures because, it is presumed, it is not problematic. In fact, the referral stage is often the first stage of multi-disciplinary cooperation and communication, and can set the scene for the functional or dysfunctional interactions that subsequently occur.

Government advice (DoH 1991c) reminds the referrer that they can make a referral to Social Services, the NSPCC or to the Police. It goes on to advise those agencies to make the referral process easy for the referrer and not to pre-judge any information that they receive. In fact, although it is possible to make a referral to all three agencies, in most parts of England and Wales the NSPCC and Police will often direct the referrer straight back to the Social Services Department, or take the referral and pass it on themselves.

When the referral is made, usually by phone, to the duty officer in the field social work team, a difference or conflict of expectations sometimes arises. The referrer often comes from a non-social work agency, or is sometimes a member of the family or the public. Making such a referral is an unusual, often stressful event, during which they require reassurance and time to discuss their concerns. But the person accepting the referral, the Social Services duty officer, is in the position of having a far more specialist interest in child protection. For this worker, child abuse referrals are probably a daily occurrence. The over-riding concern of the officer is to receive the maximum amount of hard information about the case in order to judge whether it is an appropriate child protection referral or not.

Practice scenario 2.4

Evelyn was a health visitor with five years' experience. She had been worried about the Malcolm family for several months, specifically that Susan and Andrew (two years and six months old respectively) were being seriously neglected. After a particularly stressful home visit (children hungry, wet and in the care of an eight-year-old babysitter), Evelyn came back to the office and phoned the Social Services area office, wanting an investigation and a child protection conference to be arranged. At the other end of the phone, the duty officer and her team were already very busy. After some discussion, the duty officer suggested that it was not yet time to make a child protection referral and suggested that Evelyn obtain and collect a lot more information and then phone again, if necessary. From her point of view Evelyn was quite distressed – had she overreacted, seen the negatives and not the positives – where would she go from here with a case that was causing her such concern?

From her perspective the duty officer had managed to divert a referral which would have over-burdened her team, at the same time confident that it would reappear if appropriate. A 'specialist' had been in communication with a 'non-specialist'. Whatever else had been going on, the reality of the children's situation, and how that had affected the referring practitioner, had not been properly dealt with.

Investigation

In England and Wales, once a referral of child abuse has been received, an investigation must follow (Children Act 1989). However, the Social Services Department will sometimes attempt to 'gatekeep' the system by deeming that some referrals are not proper child protection referrals. The NSPCC, the Police or the Social Services Department can all receive such referrals, and, theoretically, can all go on to mount an investigation in each case. In practice, however, the Police will only be involved in the more exaggerated cases of physical abuse, and will mount joint investigations with Social Services in cases of sexual, ritualistic and professional abuse. The NSPCC has largely withdrawn from this area of work (Murphy 1995), leaving the field Social Services team to undertake most investigations, some jointly with the Police.

Once the referral has been received by the duty officer, she will communicate it to the senior social worker or team leader concerned, who will then allocate the investigation to one or two fieldwork staff. In many areas the senior social worker or team leader will retain an active, coordinating role throughout the investigation process.

Information-gathering and confidentiality　The first task of the practitioners involved in the investigation is to access as much information as they can about that particular child and family. Social Services filing systems will always be checked. Access to Education, Health and Police files will also be requested. In Britain, Police checks reveal if any member of the household has been convicted of serious crimes against children (these are termed 'Schedule 1 offences'). If it becomes known that the family had regular contact with any other agencies (Probation, Housing, NSPCC, and so on) relevant information from their databases would also be sought.

Most agencies have safeguards against disclosure of confidential information to third parties. However, the needs of the child, via the child protection procedures, supersede these safeguards, and relevant information, in theory, is usually forthcoming. In practice, the test of relevancy and the breaking of confidentiality for some practitioner groups is still an area of some difficulty. In similar circumstances in France, some practitioner groups are legally obliged to share information (social workers), while others (doctors and midwives) are not.

The gathering of all this information will take a substantial amount of time. There could be a considerable time delay between referral and actual investigative interview. This delay can increase anxiety in the child and the referrer.

Interview   Following the gathering of information, the investigating social worker interviews (sometimes jointly with the Police): the referrer; the child; the child's parents or carers; the alleged abuser; the child's brothers and sisters; any other person with relevant information to disclose.

Although the interviews with relevant adults may be quite direct and detailed, the interviewers are conscious of the need to form a close working relationship or 'partnership' with the adults who care for the child concerned. When interviewing children, great emphasis is now placed on not leading, suggesting or influencing the child's story in any way (Home Office/DoH 1992).

Medical examination   In British child protection systems, the medical examination commonly occurs in cases of physical and sexual abuse, and sometimes in the cases of neglect, organised and professional abuse. The child always has the right to refuse to be medically examined, and the parent, in some circumstances, also has the right to refuse on their behalf. In practice this refusal seldom occurs. There are three reasons for the investigative medical examination: to inform the system about the likelihood of abuse having occurred; to gather forensic evidence for use in legal proceedings; to assess the immediate medical needs of the child.

There can be significant differences between the medical examinations involved in physical and in sexual abuse. In physical abuse the medical will frequently be undertaken by a paediatrician (ordinary GPs are seldom involved in this process). Signs of physical trauma can last for well over a week, but, as far as forensic evidence is concerned, the medical examination needs to occur as soon after the abusive event as possible.

In child sexual abuse the examination will usually be done by a police surgeon (often a woman police surgeon). Forensic evidence in child sexual abuse needs to be gathered as soon as possible, or within 72 hours of the last occasion of abuse.

These investigative medical examinations have been criticised in the past for having been too intrusive (thereby re-abusing the child), and for being too inconclusive, thereby not giving the system any clear messages on which to work. Although there is some justification in these criticisms, it should be pointed out that experienced practitioners can make the medical examination a non-intrusive, sometimes positive experience for the child concerned (see Practice scenario 2.5). It should also be remembered that, particularly following the Cleveland Inquiry, medical evidence has been subject to an amount of very critical evaluation by the courts – medical practitioners who 'stick their neck out' with a definite diagnosis of child abuse are likely to be strongly challenged in court.

Practice scenario 2.5

Michael (13 years) had already come into the care of the Social Services Department because of another matter. On his return to the children's home after a weekend with his father, Michael broke into tears and told his keyworker about the sexual abuse that his father had subjected him to. The abuse involved anal penetration and had been going on for a number of years. Michael was examined by an experienced woman police surgeon the next day. He was nervous, still very upset and very reluctant to see a stranger. After the examination and discussion that followed, his keyworker was pleased to see that, if anything, Michael seemed relieved and less upset than when he had gone in. The examination had been non-intrusive and under Michael's control but, it also later transpired, Michael had gone into the examination with three specific worries – that he would have permanently damaged anus and genitalia, that he would have contracted HIV/AIDS, and that his future sexual orientation would have been decided by the abuse. He had received reassuring messages on all three points.

It is clear that it is what happens during the medical examination, rather than the examination itself, that can have a positive or negative effect on the child concerned.

At the conclusion of the investigation stage the information that has been gathered from all sources is measured and evaluated. If significant harm is thought likely, that information is carried forward to the next stage in the child protection process.

The conference

The child protection conference is the most important formal event of multi-disciplinary child protection work. It is the vehicle through which the decision about the registration or de-registration of a child is taken, and it is the setting where the direction and emphasis of work on a particular case is discussed and formulated. It is also the place where the development of multi-disciplinary conflict or cooperation is established:

> The conference symbolises the inter-agency nature of assessment, treatment and the management of child protection. Throughout the child protection process the work is conducted on an inter-agency basis and the conference is the prime forum for sharing information and concerns, analysing risk and recommending responsibility for action. (DoH 1991c, p.41)

In theory the conference has a limited field of discretion and decision, but in practice it has great influence on the whole future conduct of a case, and its role has developed considerably over the last twenty years: 'The case conference has moved from being an information exchange to being a decision-making and service-commissioning arena' (Evans and Miller 1993, p.18). Even though the conference is a voluntary coming together of practitioners who retain the right to independent action, in practice independent action in the face of a definite conference decision or recommendation will rarely occur.

The conference draws together all those practitioners and agencies who have, or might have, dealings with the family. The ACPC is a forum for senior managers of agencies, but the conference is a forum largely for practitioners or their first-line managers. Within that forum, it is probable that the four main ACPC agencies will be represented – Health, Education, Police and Social Services. The Social Services Department have the task of convening, chairing and minuting conferences on behalf of the system. In addition to the practitioners present, it is increasingly likely that the parents of the child concerned will also be present and, very occasionally, so will the children themselves.

Case conferences, in recent years, have become more complicated processes, certainly far more complex for their chairpersons to manage. However, in essence their core stages remain the same. These core stages can be divided into three. Within each phase the participant has both duties towards the conference and rights that she can expect the conference to allow her.

1   The first stage is the most simple. It is the introductory phase where each participant has the duty to inform the conference who they

are, which agency they belong to and what their contact has been with the child and family concerned. The participant has the right within this stage to understand the same basic facts about every other person present.

If the introductory phase is neglected, practitioners (and children and parents) find it very hard to process the information and language of the 'unknown' practitioner.

2 The second and longest stage is the sharing and weighing of relevant information about the child and family. This includes information about the specific incidents that led to the conference, but also it involves a sharing of information about family relationships and the general level of parenting within the particular family. The duty of each participant within this stage is to share, both verbally and by written report, their relevant information. The right of each participant is to hear that same level of information from all the other participants present.

Within this part of the conference, information is power. If information is exaggerated, minimised or withheld, the outcome of the conference may be seriously affected (see Practice scenario 2.6).

3 The final stage of the conference is the decision-making and recommendation stage. This is the stage where participants consider and weigh all the shared information, including the information offered by parents and children. The conference then decides whether the child's name should be placed on the Child Protection Register and, if so, under which criterion it should appear (neglect, physical injury, sexual abuse or emotional abuse).

If the child's name is placed on the register, the conference establishes who will be the 'keyworker' (the case coordinator – usually the field social worker) and who will be in the core group. The core group is a smaller multi-disciplinary group of practitioners, who can be joined by parents, who have responsibility for carrying out the wishes of the larger group. These will be contained in the child protection plan established at the end of the conference. This plan will include details of future work with the child and family and may also include recommendations for future legal action.

Within this stage each participant's duty is to offer an individual and agency opinion on what the outcome of the conference should be, and to suggest what they can usefully offer to the child protection plan. It is each participant's right to hear others' opinions, to have their views considered by the conference and to go away with a clear idea of what is their role in the child protection plan.

A major problem in this area is that of 'silent disagreement' where one or more practitioners disagree with the outcome of a conference, but do not voice their objections. They leave the conference dissatisfied with the result but, more importantly, they do not fulfil their part of the child protection plan.

A second problem is the simple one of time allocation. A thorough third stage is likely to take up at least twenty minutes of a conference's time but, because of the demands of the second stage, is often squeezed into an inadequate time period of five or ten minutes.

Practice scenario 2.6

Mr Williams was a practitioner who had known the Bradwell family for some time. He did not believe that they were an abusive family. Sitting in the conference he heard details of the unusual, unexplained physical injuries that had led to the conference being called. He realised that he had seen similar injuries on the same child on two previous occasions. At the time, he had felt that they were accidental. Partly through embarrassment, partly because of fear of what his information might lead to, he said nothing. The conference treated the injuries as a one-off event, rather than part of a more worrying sequence or pattern of injuries.

It is important to state that the child protection conference and the consequent registration of children are not ends in themselves, but merely vehicles for further multi-disciplinary work. If the conference works well, it enhances the ability of the practitioners to work together and so increases the help and protection that can be offered to the child. The conference and subsequent registration do not in themselves offer any more protection to the child, but are, in themselves, a means to achieve a coordinated effort from the involved agencies.

Assessment and review

Following the conference and registration stage the core group of workers are expected to form a partnership with the child and family concerned, and to draw up written plans and agreements for the work that will occur within the next six months. This work will frequently involve a detailed assessment of the family's social interaction, parenting skills, health profiles, educational attainments and social needs. It should involve a cooperative assessment effort by all the practitioners involved in the core group.

This period of assessment is also a means of offering assistance to the family to explore the reasons behind the occurrence of the original abuse and to attempt to change the circumstances that led to that abuse. Essentially, therefore, the period is one not just of assessment, but also of consequent therapeutic input: it is where the protective intervention overlaps with the therapeutic one (see page 36).

This assessment period ends with another opportunity for the whole multi-disciplinary group to assess the progress of the work that is being done with the family. The review case conference takes place six months after the original conference, or earlier if it is considered necessary.

Primary interventions

It is also possible to describe or order the child protection process using the series of primary interventions originally derived from Furniss (1991), but then further developed within this text (Figure 2.4).

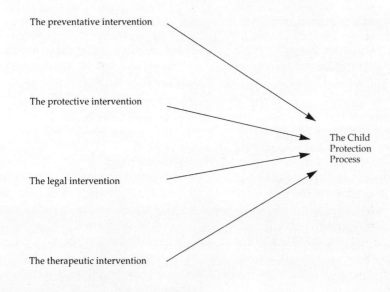

Figure 2.4   Primary interventions

The preventative intervention

This is the intervention which is intended to prevent original or secondary abuse. It will occur largely at the initial stages of the child protection process. It involves work both with the child population at large and with those children thought to be most at risk of abuse. It has become largely the concern of those agencies with a universal client focus (for example, Health and Education) rather than those with a more specialist focus (for example, the Social Services Department). The prevent-ative intervention is largely under-developed within the British system and, compared with the protective intervention, is considerably under-resourced.

The protective intervention

This is the intervention which has gained the position of central import-ance to the British system, covering much of the process between referral and conference. This is the intervention in which all agencies attempt to draw out children who may be being abused and to process them through the child protection system. The Social Services Depart-ment has become the key facilitator of this intervention, which has attracted more concern and resources than all the other interventions.

The legal intervention

This is the intervention that seeks to assist and control the child, family and abuser using the civil and criminal legal processes. The civil process will largely deal with the care and protection of the child, the criminal with the punishment of the abuser. This intervention also potentially includes all the concerned agencies, but in the main is the concern of the Police, the practitioners involved in the court system (see Chapter 7) and the Social Services Department.

The therapeutic intervention

This intervention is largely under-developed in many parts of the British system. It aims to bring therapeutic help to those who have been severely affected by the abusive interaction and should be the concern of those agencies who aim to bring therapeutic and rehabilitat-ive help to affected sections of the population (Health, Social Services and the voluntary organisations). This intervention suffers from the over-concentration on the protective intervention – discovering and processing abuse having become more important than helping those who have suffered it.

Chapter 3 investigates the ability of practitioners to span the different primary interventions, and investigates their effect on multi-disciplin-ary working.

Child and parent involvement

The direct involvement within the system of the children and families who were the subjects of the child protection process has increased considerably since the Cleveland Report (Butler-Sloss 1988) (even though these groups are still not represented at the level of the ACPC as they are in the USA). The draft *Working Together* (DHSS 1986) frowned on the principle of parental participation. But, by 1988, the first edition of *Working Together* (DHSS 1988) came out in favour of parental attendance at case conferences. In 1991 the second version of *Working Together* was suggesting full participation at all stages of the process: 'it cannot be emphasised too strongly that involvement of children and adults in child protection conferences will not be effective unless they are fully involved from the outset in all stages of the child protection process' (DoH 1991c, p.43). In fact, inclusion of parents within the process is subject to much variation in different ACPC areas and the inclusion of children within the process is proving even more problematic.

Power and influence within the system

We have already discussed the hierarchical power structure of the ACPC and the influential role of the four main agencies (Health, Police, Education and Social Services) in the work of the ACPC. In the processing of child abuse work, different practitioners hold a positional power with regard to their specialist function, where their role actually gives them an influence over a particular part of the process. Therefore, the paediatrician holds sway over the interpretation of the signs of physical abuse, the Police can offer advice on the likelihood of successful prosecution for sexual abuse, and the health visitor interprets the developmental signs of failure to thrive. But the British child protection process holds a special role for the field social worker.

The field social worker has the job of facilitating the child protection process from referral to review. Even where the process involves many other practitioners, it is frequently the field social worker who has the responsibility for the coordination of the work, particularly with regard to the crucial protective intervention. Her positional power can also give the false impression that she holds too much control and influence within the system (a more detailed consideration of the function of the Social Services Department in the child protection system is contained in Chapter 4).

Legal proceedings

A detailed discussion of the relationship between the law and child abuse is included in Chapter 7. However, when discussing how one child protection system works, it should be remembered that in most child protection systems the legal process is interconnected at several levels with the main child protection effort. The British legal system is no exception: it affects, aids, hampers and sometimes wields considerable power over the child protection system.

In just the same way that it is possible at each stage of the process to exit from the system (no further action), it is also possible to move at any stage into the realm of legal proceedings (See Figure 2.3). There are two levels at which the law has an effect on child protection work.

The first is via criminal proceedings. Much child abuse involves illegal assault of children. The Police can interview and charge in just the same way as with 'normal' assault. The Crown Prosecution Service (CPS) can process the case and the court can arrange a hearing. In theory, therefore, a typical progress of a child protection case through criminal proceedings would involve an originating report (or disclosure) that a crime had taken place. This would be followed by the Police interviewing the victim and relevant witnesses, questioning the alleged perpetrator and then possibly charging him or her with the offence. A report would go to the CPS, who would arrange a court hearing where the perpetrator would be tried and found guilty or not guilty in the normal way.

In practice, although the criminal system will be involved more frequently than in some other European countries (as for example in the Netherlands), there are considerable blocks to the successful prosecution of child protection cases in the legal system in England and Wales.

Practice scenario 2.7

In an ACPC area in the north of England, a review discovered that of the 140 investigations of child sexual abuse in the last six months, only eight cases had gone to court and, of these, only three people had been found guilty.

It seems that in the English and Welsh criminal jurisdiction, the abuse of children is a crime that is unlikely to attract the full censure of the legal system. Although some perpetrators are taken to court, successful prosecution is rare, custodial sentences rarer still. Some of the reasons for the ineffectiveness of criminal proceedings are discussed in more detail in Chapter 7.

As well as the potential involvement of the criminal law, it is possible to invoke civil care proceedings with regard to children in England and Wales. The Police, the NSPCC and Social Services Departments have the power to ask the court to invoke short-term legal proceedings (the NSPCC, in practice, seldom do so). The NSPCC and Social Services have the power to ask the court to consider longer-term legal action (again, in practice, it is the Social Services Department who will usually exercise this power).

The Children Act 1989 attempted to bring together several different pieces of legislation to afford legal protection to abused children. Currently, in an emergency, where a child has been or is likely to be abused and cannot be protected from the perpetrator of that abuse, an Emergency Protection Order (EPO) is applied for by the field social worker in the Magistrate's Court. If granted, the order (which lasts for up to eight days) enables the social worker to remove the child to any safe, suitable place: this includes the home of a relative, a children's home or a foster family. The order may then be allowed to lapse or may be followed by a series of interim orders until a full care hearing. The EPO may be challenged by parents after 72 hours, and they may choose to challenge all interim orders up to the Care Order. Parents will usually be parties to the proceedings and have the opportunity to be legally represented. The interests of the child will be outlined to the court by a solicitor acting on behalf of the guardian ad litem. The guardian ad litem is an independent social worker appointed by the court specifically to discover and then represent the separate interests of the child (see Chapter 7).

The EPO is the route that is used to get immediate protective custody of a child who is seen to be at risk of serious abuse. However, there is another, less intrusive order that allows the system to assess the condition of a child – a Child Assessment Order (CAO). This order lasts for up to seven days. The debate about this order was one of the most contentious (Parton 1991) which preceded the drafting of the Children Act 1989. However, it seems that this order has not proved as useful as expected and is not now in frequent use in the British system.

Conclusion

This chapter has described the difficult and complex process of child protection work within one multi-disciplinary system. Given the benefits of mutual understanding, complementary roles, similar perspectives and harmonious working relationships, the multi-disciplinary task within this process would still be difficult. In fact, there are substantial, structural blockages that must be overcome before effective multi-disciplinary work can begin. Chapter 3 explores these blockages in greater detail.

3 The structural blocks to multi-disciplinary working

This chapter examines the relationships between the practitioners and agencies that are involved in the child protection process and outlines the blocks that impede their effective collaboration. Although the examples which are used come mainly from the British system, the conclusions that are drawn have relevance for all multi-disciplinary child protection systems.

It is presumed by some within the British system that the presence of procedures and procedural guidance will be sufficient to produce cooperative multi-disciplinary effort. But procedures on their own are clearly not enough: 'Inter-agency work brings professionals with very different values, perceptions and work conditions together; procedures often appear to ignore these differences or assume that they will somehow be accommodated' (Stone 1990, p.50). Skaff (1988) comments that most child protection systems in the United States are characterised by 'fragmentation, overlapping and duplicative services, minimal interagency contacts, and agency role confusion' (p.218). Although the British ACPC system has been in existence for a considerable time, there are still many blocks to good inter-agency work. Lyon and de Cruz (1993) offer a pessimistic assessment of the state of the multi-disciplinary process:

> despite a detailed allocation of responsibilities for each agency, undoubted commitment to inter-agency (or more accurately, multi-agency) co-operation in child protection work, an impressive array of guidances and a comprehensive Act such as the 1989 Act, the differences in duties, aims and traditional methods of operation within each agency has militated against effective multi-agency co-operation in many instances. (p.159)

This assessment is unduly pessimistic, not allowing for the considerable improvement in multi-disciplinary relationships that has occurred within the British system. But it does bear witness to the abiding nature of the blocks to good multi-disciplinary work.

For the last twenty years the message that has been repeatedly delivered from child abuse inquiries and from central government has been that multi-disciplinary working is a good thing: 'The basis of an effective child protection service must be that professionals and individual agencies work together on a multi-disciplinary basis, with a shared mutual understanding of aims, of objectives and of what is good practice' (DoH 1991c, p.25).

Occasionally this message adopts a rather 'hurt' tone and enquires why all previous exhortations to work together appear to have been ignored! Child protection practitioners and systems become perceived as loved but recalcitrant children who have ignored the wisdom of a concerned parent who knows what is best for them!

The central hypothesis of this book is that good multi-disciplinary working is difficult to achieve, that it begins with effective communication, then moves through the stages of mutual planning, coordinated action and constructive review. These elements of good multi-disciplinary working are not easy to achieve, particularly when operating in an area as difficult as child abuse. As Furniss (1991) points out: 'The disclosure of child sexual abuse often leads to a crisis in the professional network which can be greater and sometimes more complex and confusing than the family crisis' (p.16).

Multi-disciplinary work is not particularly promoted by advice regarding its beneficial effects from central government. This is not because of recalcitrance on the part of child protection systems or practitioners, but because of substantial and largely unrecognised difficulties in making inter-agency work a reality.

This chapter attempts to examine the basis of these substantial difficulties. Chapters 9 and 10 will discuss how they might be resolved.

The individual versus the structural

One of the most frequent reasons given for failures in multi-disciplinary cooperation is that one key individual within that system has failed to fulfil their part of the process and this has resulted in a breakdown in the protective intervention. This hypothesis is commonly seen in child abuse inquiries where individual key personnel are allocated blame: 'Miss Leong was never called to account by her supervisors in respect of the two children' (Blom-Cooper 1985, p.296). This was the specific criticism of the health visitor and senior nursing officers in the Jasmine Beckford case.

There is a temptation to track down 'difficult' individuals in child protection systems, blame them for poor multi-disciplinary relationships, and speculate that, when they move on, multi-disciplinary relationships and practice will improve. In the Kimberley Carlile case Blom-Cooper's team recommended the removal of Martin Ruddock (the senior social worker) from any future role in the child protection system (Blom-Cooper 1987). Their inference was clear: in any child protection system, it would be Martin Ruddock, as an individual practitioner, who would be unable to help protect children.

One hypothesis of this work is that, in the vast majority of cases, it is not the individual within the system but the structure of the system itself that is of key importance. Thus, when the 'difficult' individual does move on, we find that the problems in multi-disciplinary relationships frequently remain unchanged: 'A system should so far as possible be able to absorb individual errors and yet function adequately ... we think it quite impossible, and indeed unfair to lay the direct blame ... upon any individual or indeed upon any small group of individuals' (DHSS 1974, p.86).

The very idea that one individual within a system can be blamed for a child's injury denies the whole concept of collective multi-disciplinary decision-making and responsibility. Unfortunately, on some occasions, even the concerned agencies can fall into this convenient practice of finding a scapegoat.

Practice scenario 3.1

Stephanie and Bernadette were the social worker and health visitor who were concerned with a difficult child protection case. Both were quite experienced practitioners and had a good working relationship. They were very distressed when news of the non-accidental death of an older child in the family came through. The case files were immediately removed; both practitioners were summoned into their respective senior managers' offices to be informed that 'heads will have to roll'. Both were invited to comment negatively on the practice of the worker from the other agency. Fortunately they resisted this temptation, and the subsequent inquiry into the death of the child vindicated their individual practice and their multi-disciplinary working relationship.

If the structure rather than the individual must bear the blame for the success or failure of the child protection system, what are the blocks within that structure to good communication, constructive planning and cooperative action?

At its core, good multi-disciplinary working simply involves agencies and practitioners moving in approximately the same direction at the same time. But why is this so difficult to achieve?

Structural blocks to multi-disciplinary work

Practitioners and managers within a child protection system are united by working on a particular case or cooperating on a particular committee, but they are at the same time disunited by all the natural differences that exist between their professions and agencies. It is these crucial differences that are the blocks to good child protection work: 'the various agencies are still working as they always have done, which is within their own terms of reference, and are continuing to contribute individually rather than really "working together" as an integrated team' (Lyon and de Cruz 1993, p.146).

What are these natural inter-agency and inter-disciplinary differences?

The eight key elements within which agency and disciplinary difference can be located seem to be:

- Perspective
- Role
- Stereotyping
- Priority
- Training
- Structure and power
- Language
- Traditional ways of working.

Perspective

One of the most substantial blocks to inter-agency communication is that each agency can hold a perspective on child protection that is substantively different from that of other agencies. This is of crucial importance, because differences in how we see the problem can lead to great differences in how we understand it, and how we then act towards it:

This means that each agency (and the profession associated with it) would be well advised to clarify its own perspective on child sexual abuse, its underlying philosophical and professional conviction about differing aspects of such abuse, and on how their perspective determines what are the most difficult cases. (O'Hagan 1989, p.63)

Agencies and disciplines take their perspective from their main societal function and from their historical involvement in child abuse. This means that, within the same case conference, the health visitor and paediatrician will see the needs of the child and family primarily through a health perspective; the teacher will view the same family through a broad education perspective, and the Police from the point of view of law enforcement or crime prevention. Perspective is also linked with the primary intervention of the particular agency or discipline (see 'Role', below): 'there are clearly different professional perspectives which are adopted at different levels of day-to-day operations ... what usually surfaces is a strong adherence to one's individual professional perspective' (Furniss 1991, p.160). Each perspective has its own way of understanding what is going on, which in turn informs our choice of professional pathways of action:

> We then get trained into our profession, take on the values and philosophies of that profession and we take on board the basic concepts and assumptions which form the frame of reference which we use as the set to solve the problems within our own purview. The tools and methods are self-evident to us but not to other disciplines. (Moore 1992, p.116)

The first job of inter-agency work is to build bridges across this divide of seeing and understanding.

Role

Closely associated with difference in perspective is the great difference in role between the various agencies and practitioners within the child protection service. Although the different disciplines may acknowledge the same aim – that of protecting children – in order to do this they come together, maintaining their own separate roles, within the wider whole. Considerable differences of role serve to exaggerate the differences associated with perspective, and there is seldom the opportunity to experience the problem from another practitioner's perspective. Similarly, practitioners never understand or experience the stress that particular tasks associated with different roles will bring. When a local authority solicitor is discussing a case with the family health visitor, the former will never have the stressful task of maintaining primary health care work in difficult families and the latter will never have to coordinate and marshal a complex care case through the legal process.

One of the great advantages of multi-disciplinary child protection training is that it allows some time and opportunity for the exploration and greater understanding of these different roles.

Practice scenario 3.2

Helen was an experienced, well-liked practitioner with many years' experience in multi-disciplinary child protection work. She attended a course that aimed to help practitioners understand the role and perspective of other agencies and practitioner groups. At the end of the course she expressed a sense of shock and disbelief: 'How could I have managed all these years, thinking I knew all there was to know about other agencies? I didn't even know some of the basics.'

Stereotyping

The stereotyping of the members of other agencies within the system is one way that we use to overcome our differences of perspective and task. A stereotype of a practitioner will include elements of their different role and perspective, along with an understanding of the type of person or personality likely to be found in that job. At its most basic this kind of 'cognitive map' is useful in that it helps to predict how another member of the system may behave. However, this way of understanding can become dysfunctional and can constitute another block, rather than an aid to communication. This is when the practitioner addresses the stereotype or the cognitive map rather than the information and the reality that the other worker is bringing. Instead of helping to decode information, the stereotype prevents crucial pieces of that information from being fully appreciated.

Practice scenario 3.3

In the case conference the Police representative was trying to get across a piece of information about a male caretaker within the family. The rest of the practitioner group successfully ignored her message. When asked why, the group replied that they knew that the Police always took a dim view of these families anyway!

This is the true role of dysfunctional stereotyping – to protect ourselves from a message we do not wish to hear: 'We hide behind the defences of stereotyping so we can feel safe in the positions we hold' (Moore 1992, p.165).

Priority

Although each agency will concede the importance of child abuse work, it must be recognised that each practitioner group will give the work different priority, depending largely upon their role within the system and the sum of the other pressures upon them. Thus, a paediatrician will probably accord a higher priority to child protection than a GP, because the likelihood is that child protection work will form a large part of the former's workload and a small part of the latter's. This difference of priority is often unrecognised and can lead to considerable inter-disciplinary problems.

Practice scenario 3.4

On a two-day course sponsored by the local ACPC, an experienced field social worker was flabbergasted when a headteacher informed him that child protection work could not be the number one priority for his staff. The social worker (using his own perspective and list of priorities) asked how anything else could be more important? The headteacher patiently explained about the national curriculum, local management of schools, and so on. At the end of the course, the social worker stated that this understanding of different agency priorities had been the most significant piece of learning for him and wondered how he had previously managed without it!

Training

'Education and training are not luxuries; it is essential that all members of staff working in child protection are properly trained for the jobs which they are expected to do' (DoH 1991c, p.54). It is clearly the case that training closely mirrors job priority, and that the groups for whom child protection is a low priority will have had very little training in the subject area. For example, even though the importance of including GPs within the British child protection system has been proclaimed for many years (see Chapter 5), a trainee GP will be fortunate if they have had more than one day's training in the subject area (and even this is unlikely to be in a multi-disciplinary setting). The practitioner groups who are unlikely to have frequent contact with abuse are exactly those groups who find it difficult to work with other groups when it does occur.

Practice scenario 3.5

Two youth workers related the tale of their first experience of child abuse work. They said they had felt totally at sea and very traumatised by the event. This was not just attributable to the difficult nature of the case, but to the fact that they felt unprepared and ill-informed about the whole process. Because they were a low-priority group, their initial training had occurred some six months after they needed it.

A similar lack of specialist training was noted by the Cleveland Inquiry: 'Of universal concern was the way in which, if staff are inadequately supported or lack special training, they can quickly lose confidence and become overwhelmed by the complexity of the problems they are seeking to resolve' (Butler-Sloss 1988, 13.34).

Training is a crucial resource for practitioners working in the multi-disciplinary system. Although staff are expected to carry out their child protection work in the multi-disciplinary arena, only a small proportion of training will have a multi-disciplinary setting. Fortunately there are signs that an increasing number of ACPCs are investing in more multi-disciplinary training events, and it seems increasingly common in England and Wales for trainers to be attached to ACPCs to fulfil a specifically multi-disciplinary role (see Chapter 10).

Structure and power

Differences in organisational structure (or how the work is organised and controlled) can prove a considerable block to inter-agency working: 'The organisational, financial and legal bases of the network of professionals are evidently very different, ranging from the independent contractor status of the individual GP to the quasi-military command structure of the police' (Hallett and Birchall 1992, p.167). This means that when a practitioner from a 'flattened' or non-existent hierarchy (for example, a GP) is communicating with a worker from a very structured hierarchy (the Police) their understanding of the discretion or choice available to the other is frequently inaccurate. In practice, this equation between control and discretion can prove to be complicated. For example, in theory, the health visitor might claim to have more professional discretion than the field social worker. But, in practice, few field social workers have to account in a bureaucratised and intrusive fashion for their professional time and activity. However, all English health visitors, via their 'Koerner' forms, are duty-bound to do so.

Even when two practitioners come from broadly similar organis-ations, the same problem of structural difference applies. Although the social worker and the teacher come from large, well-defined hierarchies, their relationships with their managers can be very different.

Practice scenario 3.6

The conversation began with the teacher complaining that she could never contact the social worker concerned with her case. The social worker (attempting to be helpful!) suggested that, if this happened again, she should contact the senior social worker concerned, who should be aware of most of the facts of the case.

Teacher: 'Do you mean that you have to tell her before you do anything?'

Fieldworker: 'No, not really. But during supervision she would discuss most of the details of the case.'

Teacher: 'Do you mean that you have to ask her before you make a decision about something in your work?'

Fieldworker: 'Yes, but it's not quite the way that you think it is. Supervision is a way of helping you make the right decision rather than telling you what to do.'

Teacher: 'I'll tell you one thing – you wouldn't catch me doing that with my Head!'

When practitioners undertake complex tasks they usually work within their own professional structure, with a clear understanding of how each part of that structure should behave and what will happen if it fails to do so. When those practitioners come to child protection work, they find that this is definitely *not* the case. Although their agency instructs them to do the work, that work is controlled by the case conference and the rather distant ACPC. Within this system, practitioners are both instructed to cooperate within the inter-agency framework and to retain the right to independent action.

Both the case conference and the ACPC are gatherings of a semi-voluntary nature, where the problems of who has the power and how it should be used prove very difficult to resolve. Moore (1992) clearly warns against the possibility of creating more unhelpful hierarchies of power within the child protection system: 'We need to watch that the inter-disciplinary team is a team and not a pyramid of pecking orders with the paediatrician at the top and the family aide at the bottom' (p.160). Within a process that aims to prevent the abuse of power with regard to children it is important not to mirror the abuse of power within the system.

One of the most common causes of complaint is that Social Services Departments seek to fill this vacuum of power by appropriating some of that power for themselves: 'we do think that the appearance, if not the reality of dominance of social services gives a bad impression to those who properly seek a truly multi-disciplinary approach to the child abuse system' (Blom-Cooper 1985, p.241). But this issue of power and the Social Services is far more complex than it first appears (see Chapter 4).

ACPCs try to deal with this problem of power and control through inter-agency procedures. Instead of any one agency having power over another, power and control are vested in the agreed, 'neutral' procedures that all have to follow.

Language

Because of their different perspective, role and training, each agency brings to the child protection task a different register and language system. One of the first blocks to inter-agency working is the difficulty of communicating what we perceive and what we mean, across the agency divide. The worst example of this difference of language is the use of agency jargon phrases which we do not realise are incomprehensible to our multi-disciplinary colleagues. They, in turn, are too polite (or nervous of appearing ignorant) to enquire about their true meaning.

Practice scenario 3.7

In a multi-disciplinary case conference two probation officers were having a debate about the advisability of 'breaching' (recalling an individual to court for non-compliance with a court order) a perpetrator of child sexual abuse. When the discussion was over, the chair asked the group how many practitioners had understood the meaning of the term. One person in the group had understood the word, the rest of the membership had presumed that they were the only ones who had not understood and had felt too embarrassed to admit their 'ignorance'.

Jargon within agencies is very useful in reducing the time spent on communication. In the inter-agency system it can hinder rather than aid that communication. A glossary of terms is provided at the beginning of this book to help with this problem.

Traditional ways of working

This block to multi-disciplinary working involves the effect of the strong, unofficial, informal rules about how practitioners in an agency expect to behave. The power of such traditions and ways of working is ably outlined by Gouldner (1954). Because these informal rules are not written down, and often not under the direct control of the senior management system, they may be very resistant to organisational change. Using my detailed study of the Coltown child protection system, I have suggested that specialist child protection teams can be used to effect change within a system and overcome traditional, dysfunctional ways of working.

In Coltown, the local specialist team were key agents in overcoming traditional methods of working that were seen to be a block to positive change within the system (for example, the introduction of full parental participation at case conferences). In child protection work, what is supposed to be happening often bears little relationship to what is happening in practice. Another effective way of dealing with dysfunctional ways of working is to set up systems that provide data to outline the reality of the work that is actually occurring. This can then be openly addressed where appropriate.

The nature of child protection work

Some difficulties or blocks in multi-disciplinary working can be seen to be due, not specifically to agency organisation or culture, but to the inherent nature of child abuse and its effect on organisations and practitioners.

Changes in personnel in multi-disciplinary teams

Most difficult professional tasks are undertaken in single-disciplinary teams with settled populations. Within these teams, relationships of trust and support can be built up and strengthened over a period of time. In child protection work, not only is the practitioner obliged to work in a multi-disciplinary team, but that team is likely to include different personnel for each different piece of work that is undertaken.

Therefore the establishment of relationships built on mutual trust, knowledge and support can be more difficult.

Mirroring conflict/professional dangerousness

Gordon (1989) claims that, on one level, all kinds of family violence can be seen as a desperate family struggle for limited family resources. Intra-familial child abuse entails conflict of interest within the family. As far as multi-disciplinary work is concerned, there is a tendency for that family conflict to become inadvertently mirrored within the professional system. This tendency has been well explored within the family systems or family therapy settings, but is less well appreciated in mainstream child protection work: 'Mirroring describes a process in which different members of a professional network take over roles in professional relationships to fellow professionals complementary to roles different family members have in their family' (Furniss 1991, p.80).

Dale et al. (1986) claim that mirroring is an important constituent part of 'professional dangerousness'. This means that, not only is inter-agency cooperation blocked, but the dysfunctional behaviours of agencies and practitioner groups can actually increase the risk to the child by disabling the normal protective function of the system. This dangerousness mirrors the dangerousness inside families: 'it is clear that such inter-agency conflicts can sometimes seriously interfere with the successful identification, treatment and management of child-abusing families' (p.38).

Differential problems/types of abuse

Each case of child protection work may throw up particular difficulties for the multi-disciplinary system. However, there are also common difficulties that are specifically related to the particular type of abuse that the multi-disciplinary team are asked to deal with.

Neglect

Neglect is an area of child abuse work which, because of its long, painstaking nature, its undefined boundaries and its confusion with poverty, can severely test inter-agency relationships. As Moore (1992) points out: 'The trouble with neglect cases is that they need help over a long period of time. There are no quick dramatic cures. Professionals seem to be able to cooperate for short bursts of time if there is a superordinate goal' (p.81). Neglect demands that practitioners within the system extend, for a considerable period of time, their positive, cooperative relationships.

Ritualistic/organised abuse

British society finds the likely occurrence of ritualistic abuse so abhorrent that its very existence is frequently questioned in the courts and in the press. This has the effect of making ritualistic abuse the most difficult and stressful of all types of abuse work. Much secrecy in investigation is involved, and the normal ease of multi-disciplinary communication is frequently forbidden to the staff involved. In a short article which described a study of stress in one child protection team (Murphy 1991) I have outlined the pressure that can be put on staff who undertake this type of work: not only can they be cut off from normal inter-agency relationships, but also from support from within their own teams and immediate family. Stress, secrecy and societal ambivalence place an unenviable strain on multi-disciplinary relationships and inter-agency work.

Professional abuse

This type of work involves the likely abuse of a child or children by a practitioner who is working with them, sometimes as part of the child abuse system. This work involves one part of the system investigating another constituent part, and the whole system recognising that child abuse does not just happen 'out there', but can occur even within itself. The feelings of responsibility, guilt and the sensitivity to criticism from other agencies can severely hamper the overall multi-disciplinary effort.

The socio-political context

Those involved in child protection work would sometimes like to see it as being above or apart from the normal political turbulence of society – a neutral involvement, by a neutral system, on behalf of a state influenced by purely altruistic motives. This is clearly not the case. All child protection practitioners live and exist in a political context, frequently belonging to agencies which are overtly politically controlled (some European systems include locally elected political representatives at the heart of their system (Sale and Davies 1990)). Even though child protection systems in Britain studiously attempt to eschew the political dimension, it does arise, often with far-reaching negative effects on cooperation.

Race

According to the 1991 British census (OPCS 1992), approximately 6 per cent of the population comes from ethnic minority communities. According to the same census, these communities live largely in industrial towns and large cities and are often poor. This means that some child protection practitioners find themselves, as white, middle-class professionals, working with substantial numbers of poor, black families. This task is not easy.

If the system becomes over-involved in a community (using an exaggerated child-protection perspective) it would be seen as being punitive, as doubting the community's ability to parent its own children. It would also run the risk of disproportionate numbers of ethnic minority children being identified as abused or placed in substitute care. At its most extreme this scenario has been illustrated by Kotch et al. (1993), who claim that, of children who have died of family violence in New Zealand, the likelihood is that, if the child is from the Samoan or Maori communities, the system will recognise that the morbidity was due to abuse. With white children, on the other hand, the system is far more likely not to recognise the true cause of death.

If, on the other hand, the child protection system was guided by Dingwall's rule of optimism and cultural relativism (Dingwall, Eekelaar and Murray 1983), intrusive intervention into families and communities would be limited, but the child might not be receiving that protection which the international community have proclaimed as its right (United Nations 1989).

The compromise solution is to try to afford protection to children from ethnic minority communities without seeking to replicate the worst racist abuses of power that are present in our society. This compromise is difficult to achieve in most areas of service. In child protection work, this balance between intervention to protect children from abuse and non-intervention to protect families from abuse of power makes this compromise even more difficult to achieve.

Practice scenario 3.8

Smalltown ACPC was worried about the issue of race. Even with a large ethnic minority community, the numbers of black families and professional staff that were present in the system were low. This was compounded, in one community, by a problem of the over-chastisement of one group of children by a religious minister. In the event, the dispute that arose within the ACPC about how to solve this problem was to show all the attributes

> of both under- and over-reaction, with opinions ranging from ignoring it to establishing special systems of vigilance over children from this community. In the end, a positive compromise was achieved where special meetings with community leaders were organised and a representative of the minority communities was co-opted onto the ACPC.

Gender

The structural inequalities of role, power and status between women and men are a constant, seldom-discussed cause of friction in multi-disciplinary child protection systems, where, in the main, women deliver the service whilst men manage it. These inequalities are particularly evident in the area of child sexual abuse, where the preponderance of male perpetrators, female survivors, women practitioners and male managers makes addressing gender issues particularly difficult but essential.

Practice scenario 3.9

The women practitioners in the South District team discovered that they were doing all the child sexual abuse work. This particular allocation of work had never been discussed, established as policy, or even noticed by their managers for several years. The women practitioners eventually declared their unhappiness with this arrangement, concerned that they were being 'dumped on'. The male practitioners, for their part, were quite startled, whilst the male managers had presumed that this division of work was the appropriate one in the circumstances.

Because this issue was seen to be so delicate, neither gender had felt able to bring the subject to the fore. But this had not stopped it being keenly felt by that part of the workforce that felt itself to be oppressed.

Politics

The belief that child protection work should be 'above' politics is a deep-rooted one. This has been confirmed in the wider political arena, where child protection work has not been a regular focus of inter-party debate. In the local government context, a similar consensus, even at times of financial constraint, is often achieved. But politics still has a way of intruding into this arena. Bea Campbell (1988) has described how the Cleveland crisis formed a patriarchal alliance between Stuart Bell and many Conservative MPs, who were intent on demeaning the women practitioners involved, at the same time as denying the incidence of child sexual abuse itself.

Because child protection work spans many areas of social concern and because the multi-disciplinary system draws practitioners from a wide spectrum of agency and background, outside political issues will affect multi-disciplinary communication. It is a convenient myth that agencies and their representatives act as 'neutral' agents of a 'neutral' system. The reality is that we all operate within the same highly politicised socio-political framework, where conflict is inevitable.

In the British political system there is some evidence that child protection work is on the point of becoming more politicised. The Labour Party began a campaign in 1993 (Hinchcliffe 1993) which was an attempt to bring the potentially negative effects of recent government legislation on the child protection system to the public's attention.

Primary interventions

One final method of understanding the blockages to multi-disciplinary working is to conceptualise the differences between practitioner groups as being mainly based on their primary focus of intervention. That primary focus can be preventative, protective, legal or therapeutic (see page 35). Furniss (1991) argues that much conflict is caused by the competition for power between these differing primary interventions. He argues that it is only when practitioners from all these different interventions come together that true multi-disciplinary progress can be made. The British system, particularly when compared with that of France, Belgium and the Netherlands, seems weighted towards protective rather than preventative or therapeutic interventions. This, in its turn, has a substantial effect on the relationships between the system's constituent parts – in particular it serves to exaggerate the profile of the field social worker, one of the main agents of the protective intervention.

Conclusion

This chapter has outlined the substantial blockages that exist in achieving effective multi-disciplinary cooperation. It must not be presumed that this chapter leads to the conclusion that inter-agency working is impossible – far from it. Multi-disciplinary work is an integral part of child protection work, it is an essential part of our working lives and our child protection task. It is also something that has the potential to increase our professional effectiveness and sense of satisfaction.

However, this must not be built upon naïvety or false optimism about the difficulty of the multi-disciplinary task. Nor should it be assumed that multi-disciplinary procedures are the same as multi-disciplinary work: 'Interagency work brings professionals with very different values, perceptions and work conditions together; procedures often appear to ignore these differences or assume that they will somehow be accommodated' (Stone 1990, p.50).

What is argued is that it is only by recognising and working with the structural blocks that do exist that we can achieve a good standard of inter-disciplinary communication and action. In the past, individual tragedy has led to the need to identify individual malpractice as the reason for failures of the system; this chapter has suggested that the difficult nature of the inter-agency system is itself worthy of some examination.

The first 'active effort' that we need to make is to admit that inter-agency collaboration and communication is a difficult process. Then we can begin to understand the differences in how other practitioners think and appreciate their child protection task, and how these differences affect their professional behaviour.

Chapter 9 deals with the individual rather than structural issues that might affect the practitioner in the multi-disciplinary system. Chapter 10 develops a positive model for dealing with the difficulties of multi-disciplinary work that we can use in our practice to deal successfully with those blockages to child protection work.

Part II

Agencies and practitioners

In Part II the make-up of the practitioner groups, agencies and groups of agencies that are involved in the child protection process will be explored and relevant issues for multi-disciplinary cooperation will be highlighted.

It has become customary to talk about multi-disciplinary cooperation, or about 'Health', 'Education' or 'Social Services', in very generalised terms. These chapters will attempt to break down those generalities by offering an individualised, detailed examination of the role, hierarchy, language and training of the key agencies and practitioners who are involved in the child protection process.

Before embarking on this examination of difference, it is appropriate to remind ourselves that all agencies and practitioner groups within a given society will exist and operate within the same socio-political climate. In Britain, many agencies in the latter part of the twentieth century have experienced pressure in the following areas:

- major legislative change
- a move to market orientation
- pressure to quantify and justify practice in terms of cost per unit output
- diminished local government control in the face of increased control from central government or from individual service units
- reduced financial support from central and local government.

Practice scenario

As part of their multi-disciplinary training exercise, the course participants had to account for the external pressures that their practitioner group had recently experienced. The health visitor began by explaining the move to a market-led service, the diminishing resources, the reduced staff numbers, the pressure to quantify every part of the service and the government-inspired shift to 'independent' trust status. She emphasised the increase in expectation of the service and the decrease in overall resourcing.

The teacher who followed her took a deep breath, as though preparing for a long speech, and said, quite simply, 'Snap!'

The message is clear – although differences between agencies may be great, all are likely to be affected by the major changes that are occurring within society. In the British child protection system, participating agencies have discovered that, as service-giving agencies in a market-driven environment, they have more than a few pressures in common:

> In the survey of English local education authorities, 50 per cent of the 48 authorities who responded said that they feared the introduction of local management of schools and of grant-maintained schools would weaken the child protection service. A third of the local authorities believe that the introduction of the NHS trusts, the purchaser–provider split and GP fund-holding is undermining child protection in their area. (Hinchcliffe 1993, p.1)

One further commonality that affects all groups (save those specifically orientated towards the law) is that, at base, they have a philosophy of empowerment, rather than control, of patients or clients. The large element of control that the child abuse system demands seldom comes naturally to these practitioner groups, who find themselves in a role that fits uneasily with some elements of their core values and training:

> it is a conflict between a service traditionally offering help that has been instigated by the client, and carried out with their voluntary approval and cooperation, and one which has a duty and authority to investigate, monitor and if necessary attempt to change the functioning of a family where a child is thought to be in danger of abuse without necessarily having that approval. (Peace 1991, p.13)

In Britain, for example, even those groups whose primary intervention is preventative or therapeutic will sometimes be asked to participate in protective or legal interventions.

No agency or practitioner group was specifically designed to meet the challenges of child protection work (except the NSPCC). What has occurred over the years is that child protection tasks and responsibilities have 'infiltrated' the work of many agencies and practitioner groups but, at the same time, all still retain other work tasks and responsibilities. What follows, therefore, is not a discussion of their general work role but an examination of that part of their work that has a specific child protection content.

4 The Social Services Department

The Social Services Department is one agency amongst several with a key role to play in child protection work. It seems that, in Britain, Social Services *is* child abuse, or child abuse *is* the Social Services Department. More specifically, it sometimes appears that child protection is the domain of the field social worker alone. The role of the field social worker is certainly more dominant in the British system than in some child protection systems in Europe and the USA. This has come about through a mixture of historical chance and the exigencies of government policy in the formative years of the British child protection system.

The 're-discovery' of child abuse in Britain in the late 1960s and early 1970s was primarily driven by the NSPCC and by certain key Health Service personnel (particularly paediatricians). However, the death of Maria Colwell in 1973 began a process of giving to the Social Services Department a coordinating role within the system. The individual field social worker was allocated a key responsibility with regard to the work done with the child and family, particularly with regard to the processing and assessment of possible cases of child abuse. What happened was that the Social Work Department was to take a lead role in the ACPC (see Figure 2.2) and the fieldworker a key facilitating role in the protective intervention. However, it is important not to over-emphasise the significance of these roles, which are substantially diminished by the following factors.

The key role and responsibility of the Social Services Department should not diminish the need for joint working: 'The primary responsibility of the Social Services Department in relation to child care and protection does not diminish the role of other agencies or the need for inter-agency cooperation in the planning or provision of services for a child or family' (DoH 1991c, p.9).

The Social Work Department also has numerous other areas of responsibility. These include the fields of juvenile delinquency and fostering and adoption, also working with elders, people with mental health problems and learning disabilities, people with physical impairment and people in hospital. Although child protection work often maintains a high profile, there is much competition within Social Work Departments for their scarce resources.

Even within the child protection arena, the Social Services Department has many different roles to play that are not concerned with protective intervention or with the field social work service. For example, the therapeutic or preventative role of the nursery or family centre should not be minimised.

Because the Social Services Department has lead responsibility in the child protection arena, this does not mean that they have control over the child protection process: 'quite often ownership and political responsibility may not reside with the same people or occupation. In fact, quite often those who own the problem are trying to make sure that others take responsibility and behave "properly" ' (Parton 1985, p.9).

Since the Children Act 1989 came into force, the power of the Social Services Department, as an agency, over the whole child protection process has been significantly reduced. This reduction in power or discretion has not been accompanied by a reduction in responsibility or workload. Because of the exaggerated importance of protective intervention in the British system (see Chapter 3) and because of the key role in that intervention of the field social worker, their profile is unlikely to be reduced. However, in the British system at least, high profile and responsibility should not be confused with high power: 'Social workers are frequently left in the impossible bind of being undermined by courts in their professional opinion, having their application dismissed and nevertheless at the same time being expected to take full responsibility for the protection of the child' (Furniss 1991, p.271).

The Social Services Department in Britain is a large, bureaucratic, hierarchical institution with several different operational levels and sections, many of which have different roles with regard to child protection work. The boundaries between these different roles and responsibilities are sometimes quite complex (see Figure 4.1).

Research undertaken for another piece of work (Murphy 1995) has indicated that there are considerable differences in the organisation of child protection work between the 115 Social Services Departments in

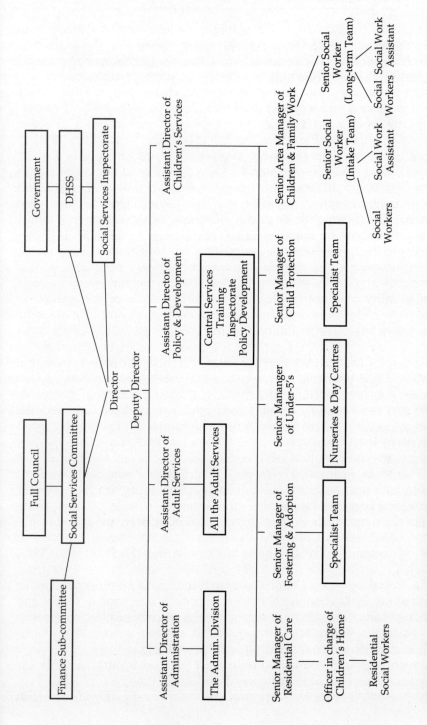

Figure 4.1 Typical Social Services Department

England and Wales. The outlines that follow, therefore, must inevitably indicate 'typical' roles and responsibilities, rather than the exact structure of any one department. Figure 4.1 suggests the structure of such a 'typical' Social Services Department.

The field social worker

Field social workers operate in office-based teams of between 4 and 20 people, under the supervision of a team leader or senior social worker. These teams will have either a specialist focus (childcare, mental health, elders, and so on), or a more generalist focus across different client groups. Those who work in the childcare arena will have a central role in the child protection process. On average, women workers will outnumber males within these teams: the ADSS workforce survey (1989) reported that a total of 74 per cent of fieldworkers were women.

Role

The role of the field social worker is one of the key areas of the whole child protection system, so pivotal is it to the work of the other agencies involved in the child protection process. This role frequently begins with a phone call from a member of the public, or a practitioner in a different agency, alleging abuse of a particular child. The duty officer who takes the phone call will inform the team leader (or senior social worker), who will then allocate the case to one (or two) investigating social workers.

As a first step, this social worker must check appropriate records and information from all concerned agencies. This includes information from Health, Education, Police, Social Services, Probation and any other concerned agency. It is the fieldworker's role to build up as complete a picture as possible of the child and family, even though this may delay the start of the investigation.

The worker will then interview the referrer, the child, the child's parents, the child's siblings and any other relevant person, aiming primarily to protect the child, but also trying to establish a 'partnership' with the child's parents.

If necessary, the social worker will then organise for the child to be medically examined.

If the severity of the situation so demands, the worker will apply to the court for an Emergency Protection Order, and find a suitable care placement for the child in foster or residential care.

The social worker will take on the task of reporting back on the investigation to all agencies concerned, before, during and after the case conference.

Following the case conference, the worker will convene the core group of professionals involved in the care of the child and become the keyworker for the child in the core group.

Sometimes the social worker will also be involved in the direct, therapeutic work with the child concerned, the completion of an assessment with the family, future court hearings, reviews, core group and planning meetings. The social worker is required to prepare detailed and accurate reports for all stages of the process.

Although there is the possibility that the work will end at any stage (if it becomes clear the child has not been abused), if the child has, in fact, been seriously abused, the involvement of the field social worker could be on a long-term basis.

From all of the above it becomes clear that the social worker's role within the system spans a large part of the protective intervention.

Qualification

The majority of field social workers will hold the Certificate of Qualification in Social Work (CQSW), or the newer Diploma in Social Work (DipSW). These professional qualifications involve courses of study of between two and four years, made up of compulsory elements of academic study and work-based placements.

A discussion began in the late 1980s concerning how well these qualification courses prepared social workers for their child protection role. Courses have been heavily criticised from within social work itself for their lack of practical child protection training: 'social work theory is deficient in providing practitioners with the knowledge, skills and understanding which will enable them to be effective child protection practitioners' (Stone 1990, p.17). Scrine's (1991) research into the child protection content of social work qualification courses stated that a minority of students questioned reported that they had had no class teaching on child protection at all.

It should be emphasised that the DipSW course is still a generalist course designed to offer a qualification that is relevant for all kinds of social work practice. It is *not* a specialist course for childcare or child protection work. Time for specialist training of any kind within the course is limited.

There are a number of post-graduate child protection courses for field social workers, but they remain expensive in terms of time and money. The number of field social workers who can be released for these courses, at times of scarce resources, can be low.

Training

Field social workers will normally receive some child protection training, either within their own agency or on a multi-disciplinary basis. In Britain there is a specific central government subsidy for this training (TSP – Training Support Programme) that has funded much child protection training since its inception in 1988. Although considerable satisfaction with the newly-funded training has been expressed in many areas, some scepticism remains: 'Much of the child protection training currently available to social workers uses questionable methods. These methods have not been assessed for their effect on individuals or for their efficacy in achieving training goals' (Stone 1990, p.69).

Hierarchy

The position of the field social worker within the social services hierarchy, is, on the surface, quite lowly (See Figure 4.1). However, if the fieldworker concerned is competent and confident of her professional ability, she can often achieve some level of influence over her own sphere of professional activity (See B below).

Areas of interest or concern

A

The role of the field social worker in the British child protection system is both complex and difficult. Since the 1970s the government has encouraged the development of the social worker's role, in spite of clear indications that this role is already too large: 'Social workers continue to have to reconcile their conflict of roles which, depending upon the particular situation, require them to be counsellor, witness and investigator' (Lyon and de Cruz 1993, p.15). It seems particularly significant that one worker may be asked to fulfil all these roles with the same child and family. It is also a weakness of the system that, at the point of investigation, the social worker is often the practitioner with the least knowledge of the child and family concerned.

It must be hypothesised that the worker's current role burdens her with too much responsibility, and that the extent and the difficulty of the child protection role can be the cause of serious stress: 'children are at risk in society when social workers ... are overloaded ... One wonders what degree of anxiety individual social workers can bear' (DHSS 1974, p.115).

B

It can become too easy for the field social worker to over-estimate the importance and difficulty of her role, whilst under-estimating and negating the importance of the multi-disciplinary system:

> It is hardly surprising then to find tensions between those agencies which have to be involved and those which can choose. Social work respondents talked of the luxury of the role of professionals involved in secondary intervention who do not have to do the 'messy bits' like removing a child from home. On the other hand, with more complicated cases, how much do Social Services seek outside professional help? (Peace 1991, p.12)

If the fieldworker is not skilled in working across agency boundaries, the potential benefits of multi-disciplinary cooperation can be minimised. It is important to note that the social worker often takes on this key, coordinating role with little training or understanding of the working of other agencies or practitioner groups.

It is also possible for practitioners in the rest of the system to ignore their own responsibility in the face of the all-encompassing fieldwork role. In the Beckford case, according to Blom-Cooper (1985), some workers in the multi-disciplinary system were content to let the Social Services practitioners carry too much responsibility on their own.

C

In spite of this responsibility, the British field social worker does not have a substantial amount of professional discretion in the arena of child protection. Her power and freedom of action is hedged about by legislation, managers (see page 72) and, finally, child protection procedures. Corby (1987) claims that these procedures can be perceived by the fieldworker as being oppressive. If a case comes to court, the field social worker sometimes finds that her evidence is overshadowed by expert witnesses:

> Thus, although the social worker has the ultimate responsibility for carrying out the assessment and deciding on the best option that should be followed in the particular case, the influence of the 'higher-ranked' professionals . . . is ubiquitous and means that medical views, for example, will be accorded a considerable amount of weight. (Lyon and de Cruz 1993, p.156)

D

One of the potential weaknesses of the very pivotal role of the field-worker is that, if that worker or group of workers find themselves under-resourced, this will have a considerable impact on the working of the whole system. As Stone (1990) points out: 'When social workers are highly stressed, poorly trained and badly managed, it is hardly surprising that the service they give is less than good' (p.62).

Practice scenario 4.1

The Midtown district team always seemed to find itself without sufficient resources to do their child protection task. Staff turnover, sickness and absenteeism were a serious problem. Many children on the Child Protection Register did not have a named worker. Colleagues from other agencies, when they voiced a complaint, were met with hostility and denial. Staff morale was very low, multi-disciplinary cooperation strained. A different management approach, fresh resources and a 'quiet period' fortunately occurred at the same time, giving the district team the opportunity to get back on an even keel.

E

British Social Services Departments are now frequently organisationally divided according to client group (see Figure 4.1). In some departments this will involve separate sections for 'adult' and 'children and family' services. Another common organisational format is the division, in some departments, between intake (or short-term) work and longer-term work with children and families. The transfer of responsibility for a case, in some departments, can occur around the time of the case conference – this can lead to great problems within the system.

Practice scenario 4.2

The intake and long-term teams had met together to try to resolve their differences around child protection work. They discovered that the intake social workers would work with a case up to the stage of the case conference (this was the point of transfer between the short- and long-term teams). However, no long-term social worker would be present at the case conference. When a social worker from the long-term team was allocated to the case, they usually spent several days trying to understand the work that had been done up to that point in time. Then, in order to fully appreciate the child protection plan, they had to spend several more days getting to know the child, family and other practitioners in the multi-disciplinary group.

F   Unhelpful stereotypes

Because of the deep public unease about child abuse, there is a tendency to blame practitioners in general, and social workers in particular, for its occurrence. This syndrome mirrors Furniss's (1991) claim that the breaker of the 'secret' is frequently held to blame for the abuse: 'Naming the abuse aloud has for professionals the sometimes startling effect that the person who utters the words is seen as the person who creates the abuse' (p.41). A reflection of this blaming of the fieldworker is contained in the popular stereotypes that confirm this negative view and hamper the role of the social worker. These stereotypes can exaggerate the fieldworker's zeal in 'rescuing' children:

Q.   'What is the difference between a Rottweiler and a social worker?'

A.   At least with the Rottweiler you've got some chance of getting your children back!'

At the other extreme, they claim that the social worker will always side with the aggressor or perpetrator:

A social worker discovered a person battered and bleeding in the ditch.

Social Worker: 'Who did this to you?'

Person: 'I couldn't see them – it was too dark.'

Social Worker: 'Pity – I could have really helped them!'

These jokes reflect the popular, but inconsistent stereotypes of British social workers as do-gooders that will either 'steal' children or side with the perpetrator of any misdemeanor. Unfortunately, these stereotypes are exploited by the media to help sensationalise cases of child abuse. As Peace (1991) points out: 'There is a sad irony in the fact that some members of the press abuse their responsibility to alert the public conscience and concern, and so hinder public servants in the execution of their responsibility to deal with the object of that concern' (p.23). Although the worst examples of this stereotyping are often aimed at the field social worker, in point of fact, the double-edged criticism of under- and over-intrusion into family life affects the whole child protection system. However, it is frequently the field social worker who is the focus of British society's unease about child abuse:

> [child protection] is not a neutral, technical activity but is riven with different values about the appropriate role of the family, the nature of state intervention and the rights of children and parents. Increasingly, welfare practitioners, social workers in particular, have been caught in this ideological crossfire. (Parton 1985, p.18)

G

It has been suggested that social workers in the British child protection system suffer from the 'cuckoo syndrome', in which child protection work topples out the other general childcare tasks from the social work nest. Even within their child protection role, the field social worker is again encouraged to concentrate on protective intervention at the expense of her wider involvement in the preventative and therapeutic areas of intervention.

The social work manager

The relationship between field social worker and first-line supervisor is a critical one in the management of child protection work. In the same way that the fieldworker is at the interface between client and agency, the first-line manager (senior social worker) is the interface between the fieldworker and higher levels of authority. The social work management system ascends from the person who leads the team unit (senior or team leader) to the director at the top of the hierarchical pyramid (see Figure 4.1). The higher up the structure, the more likely it will be dominated by men (ADSS 1989). In social work, as in many other helping professions, women deliver and men manage!

Social work managers do not only draw their power from their position within the hierarchy, but also from the fact that they are professionally qualified in social work, often having more experience in child protection work than the members of their team. Although managers have the discretion within child protection to use their power in a very overt manner, this seldom occurs. Less obvious, more professional or procedural ways of influencing practitioners are preferred. Howe (1986) claims that procedures are used as an acceptable instrument of control: 'The use of formal procedures and statutory devices allowed situations to be viewed more narrowly and in this narrow sense, control could be achieved more easily' (p.125).

Role

The central role of the social work manager is difficult to over-estimate. They will be directly involved in:

- the intake process where the seriousness or dangerousness of the child protection situation is judged
- the allocation of the investigation, when a decision is made about which social worker(s) will hold the case
- the case conference and initial decision-making stage
- the supervision and mentoring of the worker who is dealing with the case on a long-term basis
- the decisions about legal proceedings and long-term plans for the child.

Although the social worker bears much responsibility for the conduct of a case, the manager holds the final responsibility. Some operational power over child protection cases is left with the practitioner, but the lion's share is left with the manager.

Qualification

Managers in the British system will always be trained social workers with CQSW or DipSW qualifications (see page 67). Increasingly, they will also possess a management qualification, for example the DMS (Diploma in Management Studies), or in a few cases the MBA (Master of Business Administration). It is increasingly common for managers to develop along the route of NVQ (National Vocational Qualifications) and MCI (Management Charter Initiative). It has been claimed that this management training can detach them from their professional orientation: 'Even though most managers are professionally qualified social workers, their skills and interests have shifted and been encouraged towards management-bound technologies and ideas' (Howe 1986, p.150).

Training

Most managers of childcare teams will have received some child abuse training (even though it may have been some time ago). Although managers are likely to have received some general management training, they are less likely to have received specific training in the management of child protection. There is a developing literature on the management of child protection (Gadsby Waters 1992; Richards, Payne and Shepperd 1990) and a considerable number of courses available, but access to these courses can be limited. Managers in the child protection field will seldom train on a multi-agency basis.

Areas of interest or concern

A

The issue of power and control can be seen to be problematic. Howe (1986) claims that social work, and children and family work in particular, 'suffers the worst of both worlds: weak, ineffectual fieldwork and strong but remote managers' (p.162). Howe's argument has been substantially challenged by teams who claim not to suffer the worst of both worlds. But what is certain is that, where a problem exists between field social worker and social work manager, it can have serious consequences for the overall conduct of a child protection case.

Practice scenario 4.3

Stephen the social worker was not enjoying a good relationship with his senior, Ruth. Stephen saw Ruth as being over-controlling. Ruth saw Stephen as being an inadequate practitioner, who needed careful monitoring. The situation became so serious that Stephen began to take decisions without his senior's or the multi-disciplinary system's knowledge. These decisions included the unauthorised commencement of home contact for Jane, a young child who had been abused within her family. On the second period of (unauthorised) contact, Jane was physically assaulted during the contact and had to be admitted to hospital. Stephen was suspended from duty, and left the team shortly afterwards. A special conference was called and the case was re-allocated to another worker.

B

It is one of the manager's most important responsibilities to consult with and support the practitioner. However, the team leader's job in child protection can be very lonely and unsupported. The pressure from child protection referrals can be intense, and the allocation of resources often inadequate. Perhaps the best evidence of this is in the situation and treatment of Martin Ruddock, the senior social worker in the Kimberley Carlile case (Blom-Cooper 1987).

Practice scenario 4.4

Martin Ruddock was the senior social worker of the under-resourced fieldwork team who were involved in the Kimberley Carlile case. Because of staff shortages Mr Ruddock was forced to allocate the Carlile case to himself. Poorly supervised and under-resourced, he attempted to give a professional service, only to be publicly pilloried when Kimberley died.

Blom-Cooper, in the Kimberley Carlile Inquiry, commented: 'We suspect that part of the problem was that he over-worked, to the detriment of his professionalism.' (Blom-Cooper 1987, p.22)

To be a basic-grade social worker in the child protection field is not easy, neither is the position of managing those basic-grade staff. Frequently social work practitioners will bring their problems to their team leader and demand a high degree of personal support and professional competency in dealing with them. Team leaders are often unable to access such support for themselves.

The social work assistant

The role of the social work assistant in Britain has changed and developed with the passage of time. Formerly located mainly in work with adult clients, they now are increasingly active in the child protection arena.

Role

In some areas the assistant's role can seem to be very close to that of their qualified colleagues. For example, they are becoming increasingly active in managing and supervising contact (formerly 'access') in child protection cases. Although they are not really supposed to fulfil an investigative role, they have participated in child protection assessments and have been required to give evidence in court. Some assistants also undertake therapeutic work with children.

Qualification

Social work assistants are not professionally qualified in the social work field (although the role can be used as a way of getting good pre-qualification social work experience).

Training

Social work assistants are receiving more and better in-service child protection training, although they are usually deemed to be of less priority than qualified social workers.

Areas of interest and concern

A

The assistant's role is potentially very stressful. It involves much contact with seriously abused children and their parents, but at the same time their role lacks the status to really influence the conduct of the case.

B

The social work assistant's job is not well remunerated.

C

As well as being underpaid, the social work assistant has low status both within the Social Services Department and within the wider system itself. They are the 'dogsbodies' of the Social Work Department generally, as well as helping out with some of the more difficult tasks in the child protection system. The vast majority are women. Fineman (1985) notes that the ambiguity of role and responsibility combined with their uncertain status can cause stress and anxiety:

> in practice their role was generally indistinguishable from that of the fully qualified social worker. This proved to be a paradoxical, and indeed stressful position ... They were not formally qualified social workers, were paid less than social workers, and technically de-barred from carrying the same responsibilities. Yet, in a resource-squeezed organisation, such distinctions were apt to become academic 'in order to keep the ship afloat'. (p.56)

The residential social worker

The residential social worker is the practitioner who staffs the residential childcare establishments, working with the children and young people who live there, sometimes also working with their families. The residential social worker operates within a hierarchical team, the size of which is dependent on the size of establishment. The residential social worker will cover the establishment on a 24-hour basis – this necessitates shiftwork, weekend work and sleep-over duties.

Role

The residential social worker becomes involved in the child protection process at a late but very difficult stage. Children who have been seriously abused are frequently placed in a residential establishment when rehabilitation at home or placement with a foster or adoptive family has proved unsuccessful; Warner (1993) estimated that one-third of children in residential care had been sexually abused. It is the residential social worker's role to provide a safe, homely and thera-peutic environment for the group of children, and to offer individual work and care for each individual child in the group.

Qualification

This is an area of controversy in the British social work system, much debated in inquiry reports in the 1980s and 1990s. Most of the basic-grade staff in children's homes are not professionally qualified, and many senior managers, as Utting (1991) revealed, are similarly unquali-fied. A government scheme to increase this number was introduced in 1992, but has had only limited effectiveness. Formerly, residential social work staff who were qualified would usually have studied for the CSS award (Certificate in Social Service) specifically designed for residential work. However, by the mid-1990s all these courses had changed into the new DipSW course, designed for both field and residential social workers. Thus, once qualified, residential social workers can and do move to fieldwork posts.

The two reports that followed Utting's (1991) were to question the advisability of only pursuing the social work DipSW qualification: those by Howe (1992) and Warner (1993) favoured more specific, work-based qualification routes.

Training

Residential social workers have some access to child protection training, but tend to have less priority than fieldworkers, and often begin from a different starting position.

Areas of interest and concern

A

The difficulty of residential social work has increased considerably in recent years, with staff having to work with a greater proportion of severely abused, troubled children. This can be extremely stressful.

Practice scenario 4.5

Susan arrived at Twelvetrees children's home as an unqualified, inexperienced residential social worker. She was young, enthusiastic and quite popular with staff and children. Susan was allocated to be Darren's special keyworker. Only a few days later Darren chose to talk to Susan about the sexual abuse that he had been subjected to in his life. Darren's pain was so intense, his needs so great, that Susan quickly found herself in a state of emotional collapse. She took a good deal of time to recover and to return to work to attempt to start again.

B

Residential staff are less likely than their fieldwork counterparts to be professionally qualified, or, often, less likely to have access to good-quality child protection training (see page 77).

C

Staff are obliged to meet the individual needs of children at the same time as controlling and meeting the needs of the group. This duality between the control of very unhappy children within the group and the giving to those same children the love and stability that they need is both the point and the difficulty of residential social work.

D

When measured against the fieldwork part of the agency, it is clear that residential social work can be seen as the 'Cinderella' branch of the social work service, with less power, status and resources than its fieldwork counterpart. Because of this, the relationship between residential and field social workers can often be fraught with conflict and difficulty.

E

Compared with the fieldwork service, the residential social work service holds little power. But within the individual children's home a large amount of power is wielded by the officer in charge. Where professional standards are high, this amount of power is not problematic. However, as the case of Frank Beck (Leicestershire County Council 1993) indicates, an unscrupulous, abusive officer in charge can utilise this power to instigate a regime of professional abuse. This means that the most damaged children can be re-abused by the very system that is supposed to be protecting and treating them.

The foster carer

Foster parents are assessed, registered, controlled and (hopefully) supported by social work staff from voluntary organisations and Social Services Departments. Foster carers offer their service to a large number of different types of children in different contexts. Some foster carers will be short-term, some long-term, and some will work on a contractual basis. Foster carers have always cared for children who have been abused, but this role (particularly with regard to children who have been sexually abused) has, in recent years, become much more apparent.

Role

Foster parents give a home, warmth, affection and positive parenting to children who need care away from their own families, some of whom will have been abused. Since the Children Act 1989 came into force they are also being expected to take a much more active role in working with the natural parents of the children in their care.

The Children Act 1989 has also insisted on foster parents being more aware of children's cultural and religious needs. Most foster parents are not paid a wage but receive an allowance (which varies in different parts of the country) to meet childcare expenses.

Qualification

There is no appropriate fostering qualification. Very few foster parents are qualified in social work.

Training

In Britain in the 1990s there has been an increase in specific training for foster parents, which often includes elements of child protection training. The length and content of this training is not standardised, and will vary from one local authority or voluntary social work organisation to the next.

Areas of interest and concern

A

Unlike any other group, foster parents take severely abused children into their own families and live with them on a daily basis. Although foster carers can benefit from the support of social workers or foster parent groups, the potential stress on foster parents and their families is very considerable.

B

Foster carers, despite a close relationship with the child, have little power, influence or status within the Social Services and child protection systems. This is partly a result of their lack of qualification, but also because (as with residential social workers) they have primarily a therapeutic rather than a protective function.

C

Because of unrestricted contact with the child, the possibility of professional abuse is present. Foster parents also feel vulnerable to false accusations of abuse.

D

There has been much controversy about 'same-race' placements of children. Foster and adoptive parents sometimes find themselves in the middle of these debates, without too much say in how they might be resolved.

E

Another controversial area in Britain is the enlisting of openly gay or lesbian foster parents for children. On the one hand, via guidance from the Children Act 1989, local authorities are encouraged to offer positive role models for gay and lesbian children in care. On the other hand, clause 28 (Local Government Act 1988) forbids any 'promotion' of alternative forms of sexual orientation, and government guidance in the 1990s has emphasised the desirability of 'traditional' family values. Not surprisingly, local authority Social Services Departments sometimes end up with an unresolved or 'fudged' position.

The child protection coordinator/specialist child protection team

Coordinators and specialist teams are now a common feature in British Social Services Departments: research undertaken for a different study (Murphy 1995) indicates that most departments now employ child protection coordinators, and over half contain a specialist child protection team. At one time these functions were largely the domain of the NSPCC (see Chapter 8), but now they are more frequently provided within the Social Services Department itself. Child protection coordinators and specialist teams might usefully be seen as the shapers and facilitators of Social Service Department policy and procedure. They will also frequently offer substantial assistance to the multi-disciplinary system and the ACPC in their child protection tasks. They might also, according to Peace (1991), serve as a vital link between the managers of that system and the practitioners at the child protection 'coal-face'.

Within each area, the coordinator and/or specialist team will have developed their role in individualised ways that suit the particular needs of the local system. What follows, therefore, is a discussion of a 'typical' form of organisation.

Role

Coordinator

This is the person who usually holds an administrative and professional overview of the child protection system. Almost always they will be custodians of the Child Protection Register, sometimes they will participate in the chairing of case conferences, often they are the Social Service Department's 'expert' in child protection matters. Peace (1991) explains that they also serve as a link, not just between the Social Services department and other agencies, but also between the senior ACPC managers and front-line practitioners.

The specialist team

The specialist team, in common with the coordinator, will have a series of key administrative tasks to perform on behalf of the child protection organisation in a given area. This might include professional consultation to the Social Services and multi-disciplinary system; playing a crucial role in particular areas of practice (like family assessments), or undertaking particular pieces of developmental work (as in the introduction of the parental attendance at case conferences).

Practice scenario 4.6

The Bigtown coordinator and child protection unit held a central role in the workings of their child protection system. The team ran initial case conferences, kept the Child Protection Register, gave a consultancy service on day-to-day practice to all involved agencies, undertook much joint work with field social workers and some developmental work on behalf of the ACPC. This developmental role was particularly to the fore at times of legislative change, when necessary changes to the system could be facilitated with a minimum amount of disruption.

Qualification

The coordinator and specialist team posts will be filled by qualified social workers (CQSW/DipSW).

Training

These staff are likely to be very experienced in child protection work, and to have had substantial access to specialist training.

Areas of interest and concern

A

These staff can perform a 'Brahmin' function (Murphy 1995) on behalf of the system: this means that they take the difficult or generalised guidance and rules from procedures or child abuse law and, using their knowledge and expertise, turn these into day-to-day reality for child protection practitioners.

B

The presence of a coordinator or specialist team can greatly aid the management of child protection in a given area, but can also tempt senior management groups not to become appropriately involved in the development or monitoring of the child protection service. In a previous case study (Murphy 1995) I have used the example of one Social Services Department which disbanded its child protection development group as soon as a specialist team had been established, presuming that the new team would automatically fulfil all tasks with regard to child protection in the future.

C

These specialist staff are likely to possess a considerable amount of experience in child protection work. One of the crucial but difficult aspects of their role is to attempt to pass on their experience to the less experienced practitioners in the system. Some teams may find it difficult to disseminate their knowledge and expertise to the practitioners in their area.

The senior manager

The Social Services Department has a bureaucratic or pyramidal form of organisation (see Figure 4.1). There are likely to be five or six levels of management between the basic-grade social worker and the Social Services Committee. The higher up the management pyramid, the less likely women managers are to be found (Allan, Bhavnani and French 1992). The vast majority of senior social work managers will be former field social workers who have been promoted within the hierarchy. In the ongoing trend towards a specialist form of organisation, many social work managers may have worked in different specialist areas. But, from area manager to director, if child abuse is currently within their purview, it will become one of their work priorities.

Role

Senior social work managers do not have much contact with day-to-day child protection practice, which will be left to practitioners and junior managers, but they will have a role with regard to policy and will act as the department's representatives on the ACPC. Senior managers will also be involved in major decisions on controversial or difficult cases, which unfortunately, in some systems, are not rare.

A further important role for the social work senior manager is the political 'brokering' between the local authority Social Services Committee, the regional Social Services Inspectorate, the national Department of Health, and the local practitioners on the ground. Sometimes the interests of all these different groups will coincide, most often they will not. This is when the senior manager's job can become very difficult.

Qualification

Senior managers will be qualified social workers (CQSW/DipSW), and will often possess further management qualifications.

Training

Senior managers are more likely to have had up-to-date training in management skills, rather than in child protection work.

The elected member

At the top of the Social Services pyramid is the Director of Social Services. The director reports to the Social Services Committee, which, in turn, represents the interests of the full council and, via the council, the political will of the local population. The position of the elected member on the Social Services Committee is powerful but, in practice, can be restricted by various considerations. In the rest of Europe it is not uncommon for local political representatives to play a full part in child protection work. Most notably, in Denmark local elected representatives take some child protection decisions which, in Britain, are reserved for the court.

Role

The elected member has little control or knowledge over day-to-day child protection work, this being seen as the domain of the fieldworker and fieldwork manager. However, the elected member will take part in discussion on cases that go wrong, particularly if there has been a complaint or there are issues that will feature in the media. Most important, the elected member controls the allocation of resources to child protection work.

Training

Elected members will not usually be trained in child protection.

Areas of interest and concern

A

Where there is a dispute between an elected member and a social work manager this dispute will question the boundaries of the roles of each of them.

Practice scenario 4.7

In the case of the Rochdale organised abuse investigation in 1990, there arose a specific dispute between Rochdale Social Services management and certain elected members, who felt that the Social Work Department was being too intrusive into family life. One of the councillors struggled to gain access to confidential child protection files and to organise a monitoring committee of councillors who would oversee all applications for emergency orders.

In contentious areas there is always the possibility of a dispute between the political and the professional controllers of child protection work.

B

Elections can lead to a change in control of the Social Services Committee which, in turn, can lead to significant changes in policy. In some circumstances this can affect the delivery of the child protection service.

Other groups of staff

This list of Social Services staff is not exhaustive. In some areas family aides and homecare workers will be very involved in the work with families with children on the Child Protection Register, in others juvenile justice workers will have substantial involvement with adolescent perpetrators of sexual abuse. In many areas nurseries and family centres undertake key therapeutic work with families where abuse is a problem.

Conclusion

At the beginning of this chapter it was stated that Social Services Departments were *not* conterminous with child abuse. Many other agencies have important roles to play within the system, and Social Services Departments themselves have many other important functions to attend to.

However, at this point, it is important to recognise just how central child abuse is to the work of Social Services Departments, and how critical those departments are to the system. From referral to final outcome, from case conference to rehabilitation home or adoption, Social Service practitioners play essential parts in the process, and their department holds a key role of facilitation and coordination in the wider system.

Because of the exaggerated importance of the protective function in the British system, and because of the field social worker's position with regard to this function, since 1974 child protection work has become the 'cuckoo in the nest' of the social worker's children and families work. The size of this protective role can be a substantial burden to the fieldwork service, and can affect their relationship with the preventative and therapeutic interventions that come from their own agency and from the multi-disciplinary system.

Sometimes the members of the Social Services Departments appear to be wrapped up in themselves, slow to give feedback to their colleagues from other agencies, and not as accessible as could be wished. However, this should be seen, not in terms of individual or collective pathology, but in terms of the undoubted overall difficulty and complexity of their child protection task, combined with the pressure to 'get it right'. Some Social Services staff welcome the opportunity to have the 'lead role' with regard to child protection. However, their lack of power, resources and control, combined with critical public and professional scrutiny, can mean that this role is a very mixed blessing for the average social worker and Social Work Department.

One way to relieve the burden of this task is to share the responsibility of the protective function appropriately with other practitioners and other agencies in the system, using their different skills and knowledge to enhance the effectiveness of the child protection service. In return, it is appropriate for Social Services Departments to attempt to help those agencies with their own preventative, protective and therapeutic tasks.

5   The Health Service

Health Service professionals fulfil some of the most crucial tasks associated with child protection work. In an age when the technical ability of medicine to combat the major forms of childhood illness is quite advanced, the knowledge that some forms of serious physical and emotional trauma are caused by intra-familial maltreatment is a challenge and a problem for all those involved in healthcare.

Although some health practitioners undertake the most experimental and developmental work in the child protection field, involvement in this area of work is not easy for many health professionals, who discover that child abuse challenges some of the basic understandings of their relationship with their patients. Thus it is child protection work that insists on the realisation that the child's interests and the parent's interests, in healthcare terms, might not be conterminous. This bifurcation of interests is at the heart of the difficulty that health professionals experience in child abuse work:

> Technical and ethical tensions emerge when the interests of one patient clash with those of another member of the family, disrupting their normal and necessary presumptions that parents are truthful, caring and collaborative in the medical treatment of their children. (Hallett and Birchall 1992, p.140)

In just the same way that the legal structure is aimed at adults (see Chapter 7), the structures of medical ethics are formulated to deal with reasoning adults who are able to engage in free communication with their health practitioners. When dealing with children, whose interests might be diametrically opposed to the adults around them, these adult-orientated ethics are not completely pertinent.

Confidentiality

Confidentiality is the professionally constructed contract of privacy between the giver (health practitioner) and receiver (patient) of the Health Service. Confidentiality is there for the benefit of the patient and should only be broken to benefit the patient with their specific agreement.

In practice, in child abuse, there is frequently a strong element of secrecy that prevents the abuse becoming apparent to the outside world. If the medical practitioner gives a total guarantee of confidentiality, she is left with the knowledge of that abuse without the means to stop it. As Moore (1992) points out, the practitioner who gets caught in this trap will become totally impotent. If the practitioner becomes trapped, the abuse will probably carry on or get worse. The practitioner thus becomes a part of the problem rather than the solution.

However, who is to give consent for confidentiality to be broken? Frequently the child is too young to give that informed consent, and the parent might sometimes withhold consent for their own interests. In general terms, it has been agreed by government and professional health associations that the practitioner has the right to break confidentiality in the interests of the child. But, in practice, those interests are difficult to define, and the associations of health practitioners in several countries have difficulty in achieving consensus in this area. In the British system, the General Medical Council (GMC) still finds itself wrangling over appropriate guidance to doctors:

> A number of doctors believe that the [General Medical] Council's guidance should include a direction to doctors to disclose all cases of suspected or actual child abuse which they encountered.
> The Committee carefully considered the arguments . . . but concluded that such inflexible advice would not always be in the patient's best interest . . . a doctor's first duty was to the abused child . . . While disclosure of information would usually be in the child's best interest, circumstances might arise where this would not be the case. (GMC 1993, p.7)

Within the communication of a single health discipline, or within a single healthcare team, the issue of confidentiality might not cause much anxiety in practice: 'Confidentiality is a means of disseminating information around a restricted circle of like-minded people' (Rooney 1980, p.53). But in the multi-disciplinary arena this information must be shared between all relevant agencies and practitioners, and with the parents and children concerned. It is this sharing that can be particularly difficult:

There is no easy answer to this problem with the responsibilities for protection of children suspected of having been abused, the element of secrecy inherent in family sexual abuse, the likelihood that if true an offence has been committed, the wishes of the child and the duty of confidentiality between doctor and patient. (Butler-Sloss 1988, p.212)

Consent

Consent, like confidentiality, is a professional construct based on the presumption that the patient is an adult who can freely and logically weigh the consequences of the medical service that is offered. It is designed to allow a patient to give informed consent to any examination or treatment that a medical practitioner seeks to give. Traditionally, a parent has given this consent on behalf of the child and, in adolescence, the young person's consent has been sought directly. In child abuse, it may be the person who is responsible for giving consent who is responsible for the abuse itself. This consent therefore could be withheld by parents in their own interests, or a young person could be pressurised into withholding it, against their own best interests. In Britain, the arrival of the Children Act 1989 has made this position even more complex. Responsibility for consent now rests with a mixture of the child, people with parental responsibility (often parents and/or the Social Services) and the courts:

Health professionals have always been sensitive to the feelings and views of children, but the view of the child has not been enshrined in law in quite this way before. Inevitably this power of veto is open to abuse, and health professionals must be alert to the possibility that the child has been 'pressurised' to refuse to cooperate. (Shepherd 1991, p.52)

The rule of optimism and the rule of natural love

As well as the difficulties that are encountered with differences of interest between child and parent, confidentiality and consent, there are other powerful presumptions that hold some health practitioners back from full participation in the child protection system. Dingwall, Eekelaar and Murray (1983), in research undertaken in the health arena, report that the rule of optimism and the rule of natural love are two such presumptions. The rule of optimism is the tendency of the practitioner to reframe possible signs of abuse into innocuous or accidental childhood occurrences. The rule of natural love is the presumption that, if a parent holds a genuine love or affection for the child, abuse will not occur. Both presumptions, in practice, are flawed and will considerably reduce the detection and referral rate of child abuse by health professionals.

The Health Service is a very large and heterogeneous body. It includes practitioner groups right at the centre and forefront of child protection work, and others determinedly at the periphery. This chapter draws out the commonalities and differences between these practitioner groups and helps us to understand how they are affected by the problems associated with child protection work.

The paediatrician

The paediatrician is the health practitioner who is seen as the most influential in the development of child protection work in Britain and in the USA. In the USA the 're-discovery' of child abuse is attributed to the pioneering work of paediatricians and paediatric radiologists, and in Britain the paediatrician remains one of the most powerful practitioners in any multi-disciplinary team.

Some authors have gone further, suggesting that the 're-discovery' of child abuse was due to the paediatric medical specialism having need of a new priority area of work which could restore their diminished status: 'The discovery of the battered baby could be seen to reinforce paediatrics in a crucial life-saving area of work which might help it to attract resources and re-establish its previous status' (Parton 1985, p.58). Such arguments are retrospective, unhelpful and almost impossible to disprove. In practice, what is important is to understand the paediatrician's central role in the protection system.

Role

There are two main types of consultant paediatrician in Britain – the hospital-based paediatrician and the community paediatrician – both are heavily involved in the child protection process. The individual role of each paediatrician will be made up of a complex mixture of contractual responsibilities (agreed with the Health Authority or Trust), the paediatrician's own areas of personal interest, and the needs of the local child protection system (as established by the ACPC). What follows is therefore a discussion of an 'average' paediatrician's role.

The community paediatrician has the role of coordinating the screening of children in the community who are showing signs of delayed or inappropriate development. Thus the 'chronic' phases of abuse – particularly neglect, failure to thrive, disability through abuse, and so on – would often be recognised or referred by the community paediatrician.

The hospital-based paediatrician, on the other hand, will receive referrals of acute forms of child illness and acute forms of abuse – notably physical abuse – from other health or child protection practitioners.

Both types of paediatrician may have some involvement in the field of child sexual abuse, but this particular role is more often undertaken by police surgeons (see page 103).

To fully understand the role of the paediatrician in the child protection process it is important to acknowledge the key place of medical diagnosis in the investigation of abuse. The 'battered baby syndrome' was a medically identified and quantified syndrome. It relied on the paediatrician's (largely unquestioned) scientific ability to separate out those injuries that had been caused by parental violence and those that had been caused by normal accidents. The diagnosis (is it non-accidental injury or not?) became the key to the discovery of abuse, the registration of children and the measurement of the seriousness of the abusive act. Dingwall, Eekelar and Murray (1983) suggest that, in the 1970s and early 1980s in Britain, the power of the medical diagnosis and therefore the power of the paediatrician was substantial.

With the 're-discovery' of other forms of abuse, the central place of the medical diagnosis was retained. One of the most controversial debates in the Cleveland crisis was the claim (vociferously denied by the paediatricians involved) that diagnoses of child sexual abuse had been made solely on the presence or signs of anal dilatation, without the corroboration of other medical or social evidence.

If the diagnosis is of such key importance, that diagnosis can only be given by a person with considerable expertise in assessing trauma in children. This means that the practitioners from the groups with less status (social worker, health visitor, teacher and Police) merely observe likely signs of abuse, referring on to the paediatrician for definitive diagnosis. The GP is also encouraged to refer on: 'Doctors on the front line must realise and accept the limits of their responsibility. They do not have to make a definitive diagnosis and should have a comparatively low threshold of referral' (Speight 1993, p.8). This leaves the paediatrician with a very central role in both the protective and legal interventions.

Qualification

Paediatricians are qualified doctors who have undertaken considerable further training in child health. This might include a general paediatric background, or more specific training within a given child specialism. They will hold the qualification FRCP (Fellow of the Royal College of Physicians). Most paediatricians are contracted to work for Health Authorities or Health Trusts.

Training

The paediatrician will have undertaken training in the child protection area. However, this training will be health-orientated, and will frequently be for health personnel or doctors only. The opportunity for multi-disciplinary training is limited.

Areas of interest and concern

A

The power of the paediatrician within the child protection system is high, particularly in the diagnosis of physical abuse, but also with regard to neglect, failure to thrive and sexual abuse.

However, within the case conference, the opinion of the paediatrician does not always hold sway: 'Medical consultants are used to an autonomous role – giving orders and expecting those below to obey. They find it difficult to work under democratic conditions' (Peace 1991, p.127). The social work practitioner quoted above by Peace raises an important issue. Practitioners within the Health Service are used to the power and status of the consultant paediatrician, and take steps to accommodate it. Within the multi-disciplinary system, the paediatrician still holds considerable power, based on the ability to give an accurate diagnosis, but this power is more open to question.

B

The paediatrician's judgment and diagnosis in the child abuse arena is gradually becoming more open to challenge in the wider societal arena. The foundation of PAIN (Parents Against Injustice) in 1985 and the Cleveland controversy in 1987 evidenced a growing willingness to attack or doubt the validity of the diagnosis of the paediatrician. Because the paediatrician's diagnosis is so crucial in the legal process, to attack this diagnosis is one of the most effective ways of challenging a case in court. This questioning can be painful, especially when encountered in hostile cross-examination.

Practice scenario 5.1

Dr Simms walked to the rear of the court, very upset and angry. She had just been subjected to a vigorous cross-examination about her diagnosis on a case of severe physical abuse. 'What gave him the right to speak to me like that? I've been working in this field for over fifteen years and I seriously doubt whether he [the solicitor] could tell one end of a child from another!'

In some countries, notably Holland, paediatricians hold an even more central role with regard to child protection (via the confidential doctor service), and yet have succeeded in largely avoiding the trauma of the judicial process.

C

Because of the unusual relationship of the paediatrician with the Health Authority or Health Trust, where there is a conflict of interest or opinion it is difficult for the employing body to exert control or influence over the individual paediatrician. This can be positive in that it ensures the ability to be independent and exercise independence of judgment, but negative when attempting to secure cooperation in a difficult situation.

D

Within the British system, as well as fulfilling their usual role within the system, several paediatricians and paediatric teams engage in developmental work, either in the protective or therapeutic sphere. In the tradition of paediatricians in the USA, they attempt to engage in practice-based research that aims to change and improve the medical and multi-disciplinary response to child abuse.

E

It is customary in Britain for the paediatrician to play a central role in the organisation and deliberations of the ACPC.

The health visitor

In common with several other European countries (France, Denmark, Belgium, Norway, and so on), Britain has a specialist, community-based nursing service that works primarily with the under-fives and their parents. Like the general practitioner, the health visitor has a universal focus, and will survey all the child population on her caseload. Unlike the GP, the health visitor is likely to be highly aware and concerned about child protection issues and so will be able to give specific attention to those children on her caseload who are at risk of abuse:

> The nursing professions have a distinct and special contribution to make to tackling child abuse on a number of levels – on a continuum from prevention to involvement in long-term local authority care ... they are often well able to identify families under stress and take steps to provide support before situations of abuse develop. They are also well placed to identify children who have been abused, so that the necessary protective action can be initiated. There is enormous potential. (Norman and Brown 1992, p.x)

Because of her universal health focus (in Britain the vast majority of health visitors are women) and the size of her caseload, which can average between 200 and 400 families, the health visitor operates primarily in the preventative domain. But, because of her intimate knowledge of children and parents (usually mothers), she is also a key participant in the protective task.

There is some evidence to suggest that the more the health visitor is included as an equal partner at an early stage in the child protection process, the more positive cooperation between Health and Social Services there will be throughout the course of the intervention. Peace (1991) discusses one area in England that insists on joint work between social worker and health visitor from the start of the protection process, quoting an Assistant Director of Social Services:

> Links with the Health Authority are good. That may be because we as a department do not believe in the concept of a key worker. We believe in co-working, that is mainly through the work of a committed senior health visitor who has promoted the working together of social workers and health visitors. (p.132)

Qualification

All health visitors will have a three-year general nursing qualification (formerly SRN, now RGN). This will sometimes be followed by general nursing experience or a midwifery qualification. A one-year specialist health visiting course completes the training. Although the specific child protection input on the general nursing course can be limited, the input on the health visiting course is likely to be more thorough.

Training

In-service training on child protection matters is likely to be offered to health visitors. In some areas this training, as a matter of course, will be offered on a multi-disciplinary basis. In others, the health visiting staff will train on their own or with other Health Service staff.

Areas of interest and concern

A

The emphasis on universal surveillance of children's health is the key health visiting task, and an extremely positive one as far as preventative child protection work is concerned. This means that the health visitor will routinely screen the entire child population of the country against a number of health criteria at crucial times in the child's life.

B

However, the conflict between the general role and the specific child protection role should not be overlooked:

> The emphasis of health visiting is on health surveillance, prevention and education. Such a wide remit does not permit health visitors to undertake substantial, intensive casework. Time spent on unplanned and crisis work detracts from the routine nature of their duties and disables them in fulfilling their professional obligations to abused children. (Blom-Cooper 1987, p.165)

was the rather critical opinion voiced by Blom-Cooper on this dual role.

It is also the case that health visitors can be reluctant to diagnose and report child abuse because (as with their GP colleagues) they are wary of spoiling their good relationship with a family.

C

In Britain, before 1990, all health visiting staff, even when attached to GP practices, would have been directly employed by the Area Health Authority. However, changes in the late 1980s and 1990s in health organisation (including GP fundholding, the purchaser/provider split and the move to Trust status) have made the situation more complex. A large proportion of health visiting time is now 'purchased', on the internal market, by GPs. This could have two serious effects on the child protection system:

1 Because of GPs' wariness of the child protection system, they may become reluctant to fund this part of the health visiting service, or
2 GPs may transfer all responsibility for child protection work onto the health visiting service.

The whole emphasis on costing health visitor intervention is problematic in terms of child protection:

> The application of economic and market values may limit the accessibility and availability of health care and preventative services. In such a situation there is a real worry that many health professionals will be less able to take protective action in the face of child abuse and neglect. (Norman and Brown 1992, p.xi)

D

As a way of reducing the price of the Health Visiting Service, there has been a move, in several areas, to introduce 'skill mix' teams. Thus, instead of hiring a full team of health visitors within a given area, the number of health visiting staff is reduced by introducing less qualified, less expensive nursing staff. The full effect of this development is likely to be negative on the child protection service.

E

There has been a growing demand for effective supervision for health visitors when working with child abuse cases. The Beckford (Blom-Cooper 1985) and Carlile (Blom-Cooper 1987) child death inquiries were followed by the Aston Inquiry (LLSARC 1989) that was even more specific in its demands: 'to ensure that formal systems exist at all levels of nursing management whereby professional supervision is afforded priority ... Additional supervision should be provided to newly qualified health visitors' (4.43).

In the Tower Hamlets area, in the late 1980s, the practice of the same nursing manager providing both managerial and professional supervision to health visitors was brought into question: 'supervision as a means of monitoring individual staff performance, and supervision as a means of allowing staff to freely express their worries, anxieties and problems in relation to their current practice. These two elements of the supervision function can be contradictory' (Parkinson 1992, p.53). A scheme was instituted in the area whereby managers kept their managerial role and experienced practitioners developed the role of professional supervision with a small group of health visitors who consulted them about child protection practice.

A further complication for the supervision of health visiting staff is the fact that, unlike field social workers, their managers may not be drawn from the same practitioner group. For example, a particular team of health visitors might be supervised by someone from a district nurse background with no experience in child abuse. This imbalance in experience and knowledge of child protection work can prove problematic.

The general practitioner

General practitioners play a key role in the National Health Service. They are responsible for the primary care of members of the community. Not only do they possess detailed knowledge of their patients and their families, their background and the environment in which they live and work, but they also act as a link between them and other parts of the Health Service. (Butler-Sloss 1988, p.155)

The Cleveland Report sought to point out the essential position of the GP within the child protection system. Since the time of that report, the arrival of the fundholding practice has made the GP even more central to the system. However, if the paediatrician and the health visitor are the medical practitioners who are at the forefront of multi-disciplinary child protection work, the GP, with some notable exceptions, is the practitioner who is determinedly at the periphery. The GP is the multi-disciplinary team member whose contribution would make a real difference, but who is seldom available to participate: 'many general practitioners isolate themselves, and are isolated from the efforts which other professionals devote to ensure good liaison and common action in order to protect children from abuse by their parents' (Blom-Cooper 1987, p.235). In spite of considerable and concentrated efforts to include GPs in Britain and in the USA fully, they remain largely detached from, and wary of, the child protection process.

Role

Because of the central position of the GP in the provision of universal healthcare, it has been hoped that they would make a major contribution to the child protection process:

he occupies a unique position in the management of the child abuse system, since it is he who will frequently be the first to be made aware of the signs of child abuse occurring within the family, and, therefore, able to set in motion the child protection service. (Blom-Cooper 1987, p.235)

This hope has been largely unfounded. Within a given ACPC area, one or two individual GPs or GP practices may be fully involved with the process. The vast majority, however, will be under-involved, wary and quite distant.

Qualification

All GPs will have undergone the six-year medical training programme for doctors. This would be followed by several short-term specialist appointments and by a year's apprenticeship with an experienced GP trainer. As part of their general qualification (MRCGP) the GP will have covered a significant number of specialised themes; one of these will have been paediatrics, and child protection will often be included as part of this theme.

Training

Once established in a practice, it is unlikely that GPs will undertake any substantial amount of child protection training, and even less likely that this training will be of a multi-disciplinary nature. It is possible that the GP may attend occasional lectures or read papers on the subject of child health, which may include the subject of child abuse.

Areas of interest and concern

There are several reasons why GPs seem unwilling to participate fully in the child protection service:

A

The timing of the child protection system cuts across the timing of the normal day of the GP, with case conferences and reviews occurring at the same time as surgeries and home visits: 'What is a good time for other professionals and parents cuts right across surgery and clinic times ... The usual time for a consultation is about ten minutes. An hour-and-a-half case discussion is not the doctor's arena' (Moore 1992, p.171). In a recent study (Murphy 1995) of attendance at case conferences in one large town, this inconvenience of timing was frequently cited as the main reason for non-participation.

B

GPs do not easily fit into the normal working of a child protection system. They are largely self-regulated and are more or less self-employed, and they are accustomed to considerable control over the content and process of what they do. In child protection, that control is not located in one place but is attached to crucial roles within the system (like that of the field social work team). To yield power or control to a 'lesser' professional is difficult for many GPs: 'Doctors are trained to wield considerable power and make life and death decisions . . . In his/her arena the doctor takes the lead. At child protection conferences the chair is occupied by a social worker' (Moore 1992, p.171).

C

One of the problems with child abuse work, and with all family violence, is that this work crystallises our understanding that different family members have different, often competing interests and needs to fulfil. As Gordon (1989) explains: 'Child abuse arises most often from real power struggles, family members quarrelling, raging over their opposed interests' (p.202).

It is in this area that family doctors experience the difficulty of child abuse work. All their training (notwithstanding the Gillick principle of older children being able to ask for their own treatment) is that one works and talks with children through their parents. Those same parents might act in a misguided way towards their offspring, but will not maliciously put their own interests above those of their children. To begin to believe otherwise is a difficult and emotionally testing task:

> The diagnosis of physical abuse (non-accidental injury) is a difficult intellectual and emotional exercise. It is one of the most difficult subjects in clinical work, needing time, experience and emotional energy. The biggest barrier to diagnosis is the existence of emotional blocks in the minds of professionals. These can be so powerful that they prevent the diagnosis being considered in quite obvious cases. (Speight 1993, p.5)

D

During the late 1980s and 1990s, the GP in Britain began directly to employ other health practitioners to undertake work within their practice. These practitioners included practice nurses and counsellors. The involvement and awareness of these groups of practitioners seems largely to reflect that of their individual employers.

Over twenty years after the first regulation of child protection work in Britain, there are few signs that general practitioners are any more involved in child protection work now than at the beginning of the process. What is certain is that the encouragement of other practitioners towards participation at a local ACPC level is not proving to be enough to change a tradition of non-involvement.

It seems that there remain at least three alternatives for change that deserve some consideration:

1   The government could legislate to force GPs to participate. This seems an unlikely alternative, as governments have been reluctant to press-gang GPs in this way in the past.
2   Non-participation might be accepted as the norm, and child protection would not be the responsibility of the GP. However, this 'opting out' might have repercussions with other practitioner groups, who feel uneasy with their child protection role.
3   One alternative that might be considered is the insistence by government that each primary healthcare team or GP practice nominate a designated child protection practitioner. This practitioner would be given the authority and the resources to act on all child protection matters on behalf of the team or practice. This designated practitioner could either be a GP or health visitor.

The child psychiatrist

Role

The British child psychiatrist is not consistently involved in child protection work in all areas. Involvement varies greatly, depending upon the position and interest of the psychiatrist involved and her relationship to the local ACPC. Child psychiatrists who are involved in child protection systems will often be involved in assessments of individual children and of their families. These assessments may cover the effects on the child and family of the abuse, an assessment of the relationship between the parents and children involved, and the likely effects on children of proposed future courses of action.

Qualification

Child psychiatrists will be qualified doctors, with significant post-qualification experience in adult psychiatry and now, more commonly, some experience in general paediatrics.

Training

Child psychiatrists may have had some small amount of child protection training during their qualification courses, but (without a specific interest in the subject area) are unlikely to have attended much post-qualification training in child abuse.

Areas of interest and concern

A

Where practitioners have declared an interest in child protection, they are likely to be key members of the local system. In fact, some child psychiatrists have been heavily involved in research and development work within the area of child abuse.

B

Child psychiatrists frequently work in multi-disciplinary teams, where some issues and problems concerned with multi-disciplinary working may have already been addressed.

C

As Lyon and de Cruz (1993) explain, the high status of child psychiatrists can often give them a substantial amount of credibility in the court situation, but can also lead to demand for their services outstripping supply: 'More use is being made of expert evidence, to the extent that local authorities . . . may find it difficult on occasion to secure the services of an expert, such as a child psychiatrist' (CAAC 1993, p.26).

The child psychologist

Role

The child psychologist, in a similar way to the child psychiatrist, is not automatically included within the child protection system. However, where individual interest coincides with the perceived need for psychological input, the child psychologist can become a central figure within that system. If this is the case, the psychologist will frequently undertake assessments of children and families before or after abuse is established, giving their input into the case conference, the core group or the legal process.

Qualification

Until the early 1990s, qualification consisted of an honours degree in psychology, followed by either an MSc in clinical psychology or a Diploma in Clinical Psychology (from the British Psychological Society). The qualification now consists of a three-year PhD in psychology, with an associated increase in the importance of the research element of the qualification. Within both the old and the new qualification courses the element which covers child abuse is likely to be small.

Training

Post-qualifying training for child psychologists is largely at the discretion of the individual practitioner, and is frequently affected by the low availability of training. Access to good-quality, multi-disciplinary child protection training is not the norm.

Areas of interest and concern

A

Where the individual psychologist or the team become strongly involved within the child protection system, the demand for their services, from all relevant agencies and the courts, is likely to far outstrip supply; Peace quotes a Social Services team leader: ' "The disadvantages of using child psychologists is that there are so few and it all takes so long. We need them to give us an opinion of the child's psychological state. The courts see them as expert witnesses." ' (Peace 1991, p.131)

B

One key advantage of the child psychologist is that they can, and indeed are expected to, retain a degree of independence from the system and from the family. They can also, even in the middle of a protective intervention, champion strongly the therapeutic needs of the child concerned, giving the therapeutic intervention more weight than the legal or the protective interventions.

There are two other groups of staff who are crucial to the child protection process, who, although belonging very much to the health profession, do most of their work within different practitioner systems. These are the police surgeon and the school nurse. The contribution of the school nurse is fully outlined in Chapter 6.

The police surgeon

It may seem ironic, having spent some time explaining the non-involvement of GPs within the child protection system, to then discuss the crucial role within that system of the police surgeon (who is most frequently a GP wearing another hat). What is certain is that, when the police surgeon is seen to be doing a competent job, they will be very positively regarded within the child protection system. 'Dr —— is very good. She won't do anything without the child's consent. It's not a further trauma the way she does it' (Peace 1991, pp. 126–7) were the comments of one social work manager recorded by Peace.

Role

Because of their key role in giving medicals and obtaining forensic evidence for legal proceedings in cases of adult sexual assault, the police surgeon has retained this role with regard to the investigation of child sexual abuse. As well as offering the usual forensic service, the police surgeon is often the first medical practitioner who has access to the child after the disclosure of abuse. They are in a unique position to begin the process of helping the child deal with that abuse. If handled sensitively, this medical can be seen as positive rather than intrusive by the child concerned (see Practice scenario 2.5, page 31).

Qualification

The police surgeon is always a qualified doctor, usually a qualified GP (MRCGP).

Training

Although the police surgeon will have received some specific Home Office-sponsored training for their task, this training will have been largely adult-focused, and will certainly not have dealt with the general or multi-disciplinary issues concerned with child abuse. This type of knowledge usually arrives with experience and infrequent in-service seminars.

Areas of interest and concern

A

There has been some concern that the gender of the police surgeon may have an effect on the investigation of abuse and, more specifically, that the use of male police surgeons to work with largely female survivors of sexual abuse may be inappropriate.

B

The medical examination, as already stated, when handled well can have a positive impact on the child. However, this examination does have the potential to be experienced as very intrusive by the child. Khadj Rouf (1990) gives a vivid account of her childhood experience of the sexual abuse medical examination:

> The surgeon was a man, a ... He ... I felt really humiliated. I just feel that it was another abuse to be interviewed by a man, and then to be examined by another man ... He is getting out rubber gloves and bags and a torch and long swabs. What's he going to do to me?

C

The relationship of the police surgeon with the legal process may have some areas of difficulty, particularly with regard to the pressure to produce 'perfect' forensic evidence. In effect, the police surgeon's work must fit into the legal system (legal intervention), rather than fit the needs of the individual child (therapeutic intervention). As one police surgeon states: 'Our present legal system throws all this investigative procedure haywire. It is a system that forces us to be investigative rather than therapeutic. The system demands that there shall be medical, physical and forensic evidence' (Peace 1991, p.141).

D

The relationship of the police surgeon with other medical practitioners, particularly the paediatrician, may involve differences of opinion. The danger of this conflict was highlighted by the Cleveland crisis, where paediatricians (Drs Higgs and Wyatt) and the police surgeon (Dr Irvine) were in open, sometimes bitter conflict about the diagnosis of sexual abuse.

Conclusion

To attempt a brief summary of the input of health practitioners to the child protection system is a task that is fraught with difficulty. Because the damage associated with child abuse impacts upon the child's emotional and physical health, it is inevitable that child health practitioners will hold a central role within the system. The involvement of health practitioners spans all the primary interventions and includes the preventative, the protective, the therapeutic and the legal. However, even within the sphere of child health, there are vastly different inputs from different practitioner groups, from the key involvement of paediatrician, child psychologist, health visitor and police surgeon to the lack of involvement of the GP.

Although involved in all interventions, the move towards the legal intervention has shifted the balance of power away from health practitioners and towards the courts:

> If in the past child abuse has been seen as essentially a medico-social problem, where the expertise of the doctor has been seen as focal, increasingly it has been seen as a socio-legal problem, where legal expertise takes pre-eminence. (Parton 1991, p.18)

At the same time as this shift in power occurred, the internal reorganisations in health services towards a far greater market orientation has affected the ability of the health practitioners involved to deliver the child protection service that they felt appropriate. Power within the health system has shifted, along with control over resources, to Trust managers and GPs, who are traditionally less fully involved in the child protection service.

6   The Education Service

Children and young people normally spend a large proportion of their time with their parents, in the privacy of their family. This is where they are nurtured and cared for. It is also where they can be abused. Next to their parents, there is another group of people who have daily, personal contact with most children and young people. These adults look after, talk to, control and educate these children. They are, of course, Education Service staff working within the context of the school. A proportion of older children and young people will go on to have substantial, less formal contact with Youth Service staff in the evening and at weekends.

In the detection of child abuse, this ability to communicate with children, this intimate knowledge of their behaviour, appearance and moods, leaves Education Service staff in a key position to pick up signs of child abuse at an early stage. As if to confirm this fact, many child protection systems experience a downturn in numbers of referrals during the school holidays.

In France, teachers are directly connected, via the school Health Service and the Department of Education, to the child protection system. But in Britain and in the USA, the connection is less direct and can be problematic. Tite (1993) indicates that teachers have two levels of child abuse concern: the theoretical and the reportable. This means that, on average, in the USA only 25 per cent of teachers' concerns will be processed by the protective system. To some extent this is the result of the protective system not taking teachers' expressions of concern seriously:

> CPS [Child Protection Services] staff complain, for instance, about teachers who frequently report cases that are not sufficiently serious or immediately

threatening to stimulate a high priority agency response . . . while teachers have been included as mandatory reporters precisely because they may be expected to pick up the signals of abuse before they reach the serious stage, their reports are not enthusiastically received by CPS because often they do not constitute serious abuse. (Tite 1993, p.592)

This double bind is also present in the British system. Different definitions of what is serious abuse can lead to child protection referrals from the Education Service not being properly processed, or not being made in the first place. Successful referrals rely, to a large extent, on education personnel understanding the definition of 'significant harm' which is used by the main processing agency – the Social Services Department.

The involvement of education personnel in the protective part of the child protection process can be difficult. However, there is another area in which they should wield considerable influence. If we are to take serious steps towards the future prevention of child abuse, this preventative work must take place with the child population at large, within the school context. Social Services, Health and Police engage in some preventative work but this is usually of a secondary nature and is often too little, too late. The place for effective prevention of child abuse is in the school.

These prevention programmes might include developing the ability to avoid, challenge or speak about abusive situations. They would, of course, involve a considerable input on non-abusive parenting, and, if the root cause of child abuse is male violence (Hearn 1990), it would include gender-specific inputs concerning the socialisation of male children to relate in non-oppressive ways to women and children. In the US context, Abrahams, Casey and Daro (1992) suggest that:

teachers also play a pivotal role in child abuse prevention. This role is realised in a number of ways. First, strong teacher–student relationships provide an opportunity to teachers to offer guidance and support to children in crisis . . . Second, teachers may implement child assault prevention curricula to foster safety awareness and self-protection skills in their students. Finally, preventing child abuse involves a teacher's own behaviour in the classroom. Through resolving not to use corporal punishment and modelling non-violent conflict resolution, educators can create an environment conducive to a child's well-being. (p.229)

Even though prevention programmes may be more commonly employed in the US context, Abrahams, Casey and Daro claim that the inability of many states to renounce physical force hampers the effectiveness of these programmes. In the British context, physical punishment in schools (though not in the family) has been disallowed for some time. This automatically offers teaching staff the chance to model non-violent conflict resolution.

The British Education Service (in the form of individual departments and staff) have taken part in much effective child protection work in the past twenty years. However, this has been organised on an individual departmental and school basis, rather than within a nationally coordinated scheme (as with the French system). In the late 1980s and early 1990s the service has moved to a position of taking on a much more organised approach to child protection work. This was due, to a large extent, to the Department for Education and Science (DES) Circular 4/88 (DES 1988) on child protection (this circular is due to be reviewed and revised in 1995). The circular established, for the first time, the nationally recommended approach to child protection in the Education Service, but did not provide any resources to finance these changes.

Its recommendations included:

- the designation of a senior Local Education Authority (LEA) official to act as the departmental child protection coordinator
- the selection of a member of staff within each school as child protection coordinator and facilitator (the designated teacher)
- the confirmation that LEA and ACPC procedures should be followed in all circumstances, by all branches of the Education Service.

The circular attempted to address the fact that, up until that date, child protection had been a generally low-priority task for all denominations of staff. By giving specific responsibilities, it sought to raise the profile of child protection within schools.

Unfortunately, this central directive was issued at a time when Local Management of Schools (LMS) was encouraging a more individualised response to the external environment. The government also failed to allow any extra resources to cover this increased workload. In a survey of child protection systems (Hinchcliffe 1993): '50 per cent of the 48 authorities responding said that they feared the introduction of Local Management of Schools . . . would weaken the child protection service.' One respondent to the survey complained: ' "Power is now so diffused – we cannot negotiate individually with head teachers, governors, education department staff – it is frequently impossible to see how schools reluctant to abide by agreed procedures and good child protection practice, can be forced to do so' (p.2).

The threat of decentralisation in education is substantial, but what the survey fails to realise is that most child protection cooperation in Britain is voluntary to begin with. This cooperation rests on the ability of agencies and coordinating bodies to persuade practitioners and agencies to play their full part in the process.

In this chapter we discuss the differing child protection tasks within the Education Service (see Figure 6.1), commenting on role, qualification, training, and areas of interest and concern.

The governor

In the British system, the role of governor in schools has become much more onerous and potentially powerful since the education reforms of the 1980s. In attempting to increase the power of the consumer and decrease the power of the LEA, governors have been given much more influence within the education system.

Role

Local Management of Schools leaves many policy-making decisions in the hands of governing bodies, rather than in the hands of the local authority Education Department. This means, at least in theory, that governors oversee all aspects of child protection work within schools. Having said this, the actual power within a governing body can often be seen to lie with the 'professional' rather than 'amateur' members of that body. This means, in effect, that governors may have little influence over day-to-day child protection practice, but much more influence over wider school policy. This can include:

- the development of 'whole school policies' that would include child protection as one element
- all programmes within school that attempt to introduce a preventative or educational input on child abuse into the curriculum
- dealing with professional abuse (the abuse of children by a member of staff) in their capacity as employers, and dealing with any complaints with regard to the child protection system within the school.

Qualification

Most school governors will have no professional qualification in education. In Britain there is no appropriate qualification to be a governor. However, it is worth remembering that, on most governing bodies, some governors will be teacher-governors or will have other professional qualifications. Headteachers and representatives (political and professional) from LEAs can also sit on the governing body.

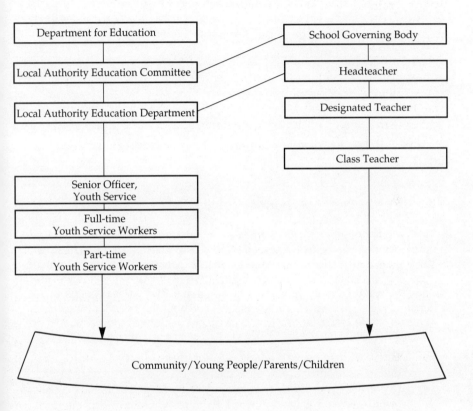

Figure 6.1   The Education Service

Training

Because of their increased role and responsibility in the wider field of LMS, governors currently receive more training than they have done in the past. It would not be usual, however, for this training to include an input on child protection. In this matter, most governors will have a layperson's knowledge about the subject area.

Areas of interest or concern

A

The largest problem area is that of increased responsibility without appropriate child protection training. This can leave governors in acutely difficult situations.

Practice scenario 6.1

In a small primary school in the west of England, these issues became most apparent in a case of alleged professional abuse by the headteacher. The governing body found themselves in a position of having to protect the interests of the children, the parents, the staff group, the headteacher and the wider community, without having any training or knowledge about child abuse. They also found themselves without the benefit of their main adviser – the headteacher. Not surprisingly, therefore, they experienced the whole situation as being extremely fraught, emotive and difficult to deal with.

B

School governors are labouring under a significantly increased workload that relates mainly to physical and financial provision for the school. This inevitably pushes other matters, including child protection, to the bottom of their agenda.

The headteacher

As both the general manager of the school and the chief adviser and facilitator of the governing body, the headteacher is potentially the most powerful force within a school. The reforms of the 1980s and 1990s in the education system in Britain, by increasing parent and governor power at the expense of the local authority, effectively mean that head-teachers are less controlled (and supported) by the centre. It follows, therefore, that the headteacher's approach to child protection work can be vital in determining the school's attitude towards the problem.

In this regard, British headteachers are very similar to their counter-parts (known as principals) in the USA. Tite (1993) comments on the key role that principals have in deciding the seriousness of a given set of circumstances: 'Besides individual classroom circumstances, often teachers' personal ambivalences are resolved through discussions with their principals. Depending on their response, principals can turn minor concerns into a full-fledged case, they can dismiss the teachers' sus-picions as so much nonsense, or they can choose some middle ground between the two' (p.600). This powerful position is replicated within the British system (see Practice scenario 6.3).

Role

Many headteachers are also 'designated teachers'. This leaves them doubly powerful in the child protection field (see page 115). Even if the headteacher is not the designated teacher, his or her role in deciding policy and practice with regard to child protection, supervising day-to-day child protection work and prioritising child protection training is crucial in deciding how a particular establishment will respond to the challenge of child protection work.

Qualification

The vast majority of headteachers will hold an appropriate teaching qualification, a Certificate in Education (Cert Ed), degree in education (BEd), or postgraduate certificate (PGCE). On teacher qualification courses there is a significant input on pastoral care, with a lesser amount of input on child protection. Some have claimed that this input is more than adequate (Thatcher 1990), but some staff find themselves poorly prepared for their role in the child protection system.

Training

If the headteacher has a specific interest in child protection, or is a designated teacher under Circular 4/88, he or she is likely to have undertaken a limited amount of child protection training. If not, then it is possible for the headteacher to have had no training at all in this area.

Areas of interest and concern

A

As general manager of the school, it is the headteacher's responsibility to monitor the running of the school and to oversee the major organisational and legislative changes that have been introduced within the last two decades (see page 123). These changes have brought a new, utilitarian, commodity focus to the system that does not easily fit with wider pastoral concerns that include child abuse. This being the case, child protection work cannot be seen by most headteachers as a top priority and, in a small number of cases, can be seen as a downright threat or nuisance.

Practice scenario 6.2

Mr Case, a headteacher, had phoned his education social worker for advice: 'I've received an invitation to the Mellor case conference. Am I legally obliged to attend?'

'No, but the procedures, the ACPC and *Working Together* all recommend . . . '

'Am I legally obliged to go?'

'No, but . . . '

'Thank you, I've got much more important things to do.'

B

For a variety of reasons, some headteachers can deny that child abuse touches the children or families that they work with (this is sometimes called the 'leafy suburbs syndrome'), falsely presuming that child abuse does not affect the middle classes. If this is the case, it is probable that the school will be engaging in what Dingwall, Eekelaar and Murray (1983) have termed the 'rule of optimism'. This means that all physical, emotional, verbal or behavioural signs of abuse will be reframed as having a legitimate explanation. Thus it will be very difficult for child protection matters to be recognised and addressed within the school.

Practice scenario 6.3

Sophie's class teacher and the school's designated teacher had been monitoring her for some time. They were worried: something was definitely not right. Then Sophie talked to her class teacher, giving her some extra information about her home life that made her even more worried about the likelihood of Sophie being abused.

The class teacher and the designated teacher, after discussion, were sure that she should be referred through child protection procedures. The headteacher was very worried, unconvinced about the truth of what Sophie had said, very concerned about spoiling the school's relationship with her parents and at getting the school a bad reputation. The headteacher refused to make the referral.

After much heart-searching, the class teacher and designated teacher decided that they had to 'go above' the headteacher's authority. Fortunately, the headteacher had also considered his position and had changed his mind. The referral was made in the normal way.

The designated teacher

This specialist role within each school has been introduced by Circular 4/88. In some areas, heads and deputy heads are invariably the designated worker. In others, ordinary teachers who are interested in the subject area will volunteer for the job. There are advantages and disadvantages to both alternatives.

Role

It is the designated teacher's role to monitor child protection work within the school, to advise and assist other staff members with child protection work, to disseminate appropriate information to the staff group and to liaise with external agencies.

Qualification

The designated teacher will usually hold an appropriate teaching qualification (see 'The headteacher'). Extra qualifications in child protection work are not widely available for teaching staff in British schools.

Training

Designated teachers will usually have undertaken a short introductory course that deals with their child protection responsibilities. Some areas have introduced regular top-up meetings for designated teachers. According to Circular 4/88: 'Such training should provide for awareness and recognition of child abuse, detailed knowledge of the LEA's procedures for dealing with individual cases, and the identification of those officers within the statutory agencies with whom the teacher may need to liaise' (DES 1988).

Areas of interest or concern

A

If a headteacher or deputy undertakes the designated teacher task, they may bring to that task the influence associated with their status within the school hierarchy. However, because of the burden of other priorities, it is possible that child protection work receives less priority than it requires.

B

Conversely, if a basic-grade teacher takes on the designated teacher role, it is possible that they could devote more time and attention to child protection work. However, it is also possible that the child protection work would attract a lower status in the school because of this.

C

In larger schools, the designated teacher's liaison role can be difficult as the total number of staff and children concerned can be very considerable.

The teacher

The majority of the work undertaken in child protection in the classroom will be in the domain of the class teacher.

Role

It is the role of the classroom teacher to take primary responsibility for the identification of children who may be being abused, and the recognition of physical or behavioural signs of that abuse within the individual child. Sometimes this role will then extend to presenting the school's information to a case conference, and even to joining the core professional group that attempts to carry out a programme of work with the child.

Qualification

Most teaching staff within the British state system will hold an appropriate teaching qualification (see 'The headteacher'). The time that is spent on initial teacher training on issues of child abuse is relatively low. Circular 4/88 attempted to rectify this: 'the Secretary of State nevertheless expects that this preparation (for pastoral responsibilities) will include awareness and recognition of child abuse, and the appropriate procedures as outlined in this Circular' (DES 1988).

Training

Some areas have established programmes of training for whole staff groups, and others have developed multi-disciplinary training programmes that include teachers. However, in some parts of the country, teachers can still receive no child protection training at all.

Areas of interest and concern

A

To have the major responsibility for recognition and referral without having the benefit of any training input poses a great difficulty for teachers. This difficulty in accessing relevant training is exacerbated by the lack of financial provision for staff cover for child protection training.

B

A teacher who has a conflict with her headteacher in a child protection matter will have difficulty in taking separate or independent action, as the gap in power and knowledge between them is likely to be high (see Practice scenario 6.3). The issue of direct access of teachers to other practitioners in the child protection system has been a controversial one for at least twenty years: 'The only question at issue is whether this responsibility may on occasions be delegated to the class teacher ... we imagine that many class teachers would be well able to exercise discretion in such referrals' (DHSS 1974. p.67). Tite (1993) has also indicated that direct access in the US context is not common practice.

C

There can be a perceived element of role conflict for the teacher in the protective part of child protection work. This concerns the debate about their true role as educators, which some believe should not include the child abuse element.

D

The pressure of work and organisational change in the British education system, largely imposed from above, does not only affect governors and headteachers, it has also put a considerable amount of pressure on teaching staff. This can lead to pastoral or non-curricular activity taking a lower priority.

The school nurse

Although the School Nursing Service is controlled, managed and funded by the Health Service, it is included in this chapter because it is still an essential part of the care that a child receives in school. Either based totally in school or offering a visiting service to schools from a health centre base, the school nurse provides the link between Health Service, child, parent and school. The school nurse will be concerned with preventative and reactive healthcare for all children of school age.

Role

The school nurse has a general recognition and referral role within child protection. As part of her job she will screen all children in school in certain health areas and may talk with children about personal health issues in a non-threatening way. This approach can help children who wish to begin to talk about the abuse that they have undergone. School nurses also have the distinct advantage of working on a one-to-one basis rather than in a large group.

Practice scenario 6.4

Joanne had broken down and sobbed in the classroom. Her teacher had been very concerned, but was conscious that the other 34 children were looking on. She took Joanne to the school nurse. The school nurse knew her well; Joanne felt safe with her. At the end of another long period of crying, Joanne began to tell her story involving serious sexual abuse which had been going on for several years.

As well as being involved in the protective part of child protection work, the school nurse can be a key player in any preventative initiatives within school.

Qualification

School nurses are Registered Nurses (RGNs, formerly SRNs), who have done an extra 6–12 months' course on child health and school nursing. Child protection does not make up a major part of this training.

Training

School nurses, like teachers, can sometimes lack priority for child protection training within their service.

Areas of interest and concern

A

School nurses are still affected by narrow stereotypes that exclusively link them to head lice and school medicals. This conceals their very wide and important child health brief.

B

The school nurse is in the difficult position of being the only healthcare professional in an education establishment. She does not have the advantage of the health visitor's independence of action, but feels pressure to fit in with the larger culture of the school and the head-teacher: 'School nurses feel very vulnerable because they are often not backed up by the teachers' (Peace 1991, p.133).

C

The restructuring of the Health and Education Services in Britain in the late 1980s and 1990s has left the school nurse in a potentially vulnerable situation. With the increased pressure on the Health Authority to achieve monetary compensation for all services that they provide, and the pressure on individual schools to reduce expenditure on all but essential educational priorities, the School Nursing Service is in a particularly difficult position.

The education social worker (education welfare officer)

This is the part of the Education Service that seeks to extend the concern of the school beyond the school environment and into the child's family and community. The Education Social Worker (ESW) service itself has undergone a change of role and orientation, moving from a concentration on school attendance to a wider social work role with pupils and their families.

Role

The education social worker is likely to have two main points of contact with child abuse: the recognition of abuse in a family within which the worker is already involved, or where the ESW acts as an adviser to other education staff on child abuse matters that occur within school.

The worker would not be required to undertake any child abuse investigations, nor to 'process' the case on behalf of the school. But she does frequently give advice, can refer a case directly to Social Services and, on occasion, works jointly with the Social Services Department staff.

Qualification

The appropriate qualification for education social workers is the Diploma in Social Work (DipSW, formerly CQSW), the same qualification as field, residential and probation social workers. A large proportion of staff have not been given the opportunity to become qualified.

Training

Because of the lack of basic qualification training, it would seem logical that education social workers should receive a substantial amount of in-service training on child protection issues. Frequently, however, the ESW service suffers from child protection's relatively low priority in the wider education system. In some areas training can be quite meagre.

Areas of interest and concern

As with the school nurse, the education social worker in Britain is affected by a narrow stereotype – the 'wag person' who is only interested in truancy. This stereotype fails to recognise their important role in many pastoral issues, including child protection.

The youth worker

In former times, child protection matters were not seen as being particularly relevant to Youth Service staff. It was presumed that the majority of abuse (particularly physical abuse) affected a younger age group than the service was accustomed to dealing with.

With the growing public awareness of child sexual abuse that began in the mid-1980s, knowledge about this area of abuse became very relevant to the youth worker. It appeared that a growing number of young people seemed to be choosing Youth Service staff to talk to about the sexual abuse that they had suffered. This meant that Youth Service staff had to be included in the system: 'new professionals who had only marginal roles in physical abuse such as teachers and youth workers become central to the task and need to be fully integrated into the professional network' (Furniss 1991, p.xviii).

Role

The youth worker's role is simple in scope but difficult to enact: it is to be open to talk to and support young people who choose to discuss or seek help with abusive situations, and then to refer the matter to the investigating agency, whilst still offering support to the young person.

Qualification

There is a bifurcation of qualification and of status within the Youth Service. The minority of Youth Service staff will be full-time staff, a proportion of whom will hold the two-year Diploma in Youth and Community Work. The majority of staff in the service will be part-time staff, a proportion of whom will have completed an introductory basic course in Youth Work.

Training

In neither of the above courses does child protection figure significantly. The Youth Service, in some areas, also suffers from a lack of in-service child protection training.

Areas of interest and concern

A   Confidentiality

One of the cornerstones of youth work is the ability to offer to the young person a totally confidential relationship. However, in child protection situations, total confidentiality is impossible to offer and, if given, is likely to do little for the child and less for the worker: 'Therapists who out of a misunderstood therapeutic paradigm of confidentiality want to safeguard confidentiality for the child and the family realise often and only too late that they have joined the family system of secrecy which leaves the child unprotected' (Furniss 1991, p.95). This conflict between confidentiality and child protection is reflected in Circular 4/88: 'Much youth work depends for its effectiveness on the quality of individual relationships based on confidentiality, but ultimately the appropriate agencies must be informed of suspected or identified abuse' (DES 1988).

B

The division between full- and part-time workers, so pronounced in the Youth Service, is likely to be counter-productive to good child protection work. The part-time workers are more likely to have close contact with young people, but the full-time workers are likely to have more access to training and to the system itself (see Practice scenario 3.5, page 48).

Conclusion

In the last quarter of the twentieth century the education system in Britain has undergone many major changes that have substantially altered the service itself and the role of its individual staff members. These changes have not been within the control of the teaching profession; many have been introduced in the face of their opposition. The Education Service has undergone a 'value for money' revolution that includes the devolution of budgetary control to the school level, but also the reduction of overall expenditure in many areas of the work.

The Youth Service has also suffered from the reduction in the local authority's ability to fund its services. Where all is quantified and costed, the value of a child protection service is difficult to assess. The moves towards standardisation and quantification in school curriculum and pupil attainment cannot hope to be matched by the more complicated areas of pastoral care or social and emotional development. In the same way the effectiveness of child protection systems in school is hard to assess in quantitative terms.

At a time when DES Circular 4/88 should have been enhancing the child protection service in schools, that same service is being severely hampered by other non-associated developments in the education field. In the increasing attempt to cost, quantify and improve measurable attainments in all areas within school, the position of child protection will remain vulnerable. It is extremely difficult to measure outcome accurately, or assess cost per unit outcome, in child protection work. It is also extremely difficult to measure the effectiveness of good prevention programmes – whose results may only become clear after the child leaves the school.

Local Management of Schools has reduced the Education Authority's ability to make child protection a priority within school. When a governing body is busy worrying about the cost of buildings, materials, external services and where the next teacher is coming from, they cannot be blamed for neglecting an area that might only affect a small number of pupils.

Proper prevention needs planning; it needs a strategy that goes beyond the individual school. Identification of child abuse needs training, adequate support and a good system of referral: 'Teachers ... and others working with children must have enough confidence to know how to respond. That means proper training for all of those who come into contact with children' (Thatcher 1990).

In spite of these very real difficulties, most schools take their child abuse role very seriously, have developed comprehensive whole-school policies in this area, and some are also developing practical programmes of prevention within the classroom.

7 The legal system and related practitioners

With the 're-discovery' of child physical abuse in the USA and Britain in the 1960s, it was not immediately apparent that the legal system would have a central role to play in the new process. The 'battered baby syndrome' was a medical one, to be treated by the child protection system rather than argued in the court. In point of fact, in the USA, the legal system became involved relatively swiftly, with legislation to make professional referral of child abuse compulsory. In England and Wales the main piece of relevant legislation, the Children and Young Persons Act 1969, was on the statute book before the full re-discovery of physical abuse and remained in place until the arrival of the Children Act 1989. The latter served to make the whole legal system far more central to the child protection process.

That the legal system has gained in influence over the child protection process is not in doubt, but that this legal influence will necessarily lead, in the future, to better child protection decisions being taken, is a point of some debate. The crucial 'no order' concept that was introduced by the Children Act was designed to shield a large number of children from the harmful effects of being included in the court process. However, paradoxically, once included within its scope, this same process was to have even more control over the child's future.

Child protection work does not hold its own separate identity within the English and Welsh legal process, but exists within that process, affected by the customs, rules and perspectives which were designed to encompass very different types of problems. The campaign for a Family Court in the 1980s – a court that would explicitly devote itself to the particular issues that affect children and families – was an attempt to establish a specialised, separate entity within the court system. In the end this campaign was unsuccessful.

However, the Children Act 1989 did accomplish several significant changes in the law relating to care of children: it collated and simplified much of the relevant child and family law that was already in existence; it introduced several key new concepts – parental responsibility, significant harm, no delay and paramountcy of children's interests; it instituted a new partnership in child protection cases between the different levels of the court system (Magistrate's Court, County Court and High Court); it set up a series of committees that would enable feedback to be obtained about the working of the Act and other child law issues, and finally it instituted comprehensive training programmes for court practitioners on the working and philosophy of the new act: 'They must have received special training designed for the Act before undertaking any of the work ... it is essential that all levels of the judiciary involved in family proceedings have a firm commitment to the ideals and philosophy of the Act' (CAAC 1992, p.10).

In spite of this impressive move towards major reform, some factors remain which inhibit the ability of the legal process to deal fully with the specific issues that arise in child protection matters.

The public versus the private domain

In the main, the law aims to regulate public behaviour, or behaviour which occurs in the public domain. Child abuse often occurs behind closed doors in the privacy of the family. The law finds this type of private, familial interaction extremely difficult to control or to pass judgment upon.

Practice scenario 7.1

A father came to court, having killed his eight-week-old child, and pleaded guilty to manslaughter. The judge gave a suspended sentence, commenting in his summing up that the man's partner had already forgiven him for what had happened. The implication was clear – what had occurred was more a private familial tragedy than a serious public crime.

Patriarchy and the law

This difficulty is exaggerated by the fact that in some circumstances, according to Gordon (1989), child abuse can be seen not as an aberration of family life but merely an exaggeration of relationships within the family – more particularly, an exaggeration of the power of the male parent within the family: 'The incestuous pattern, again, is an exaggeration of the patriarchal pattern, not a reversal of it' (Gordon 1989, p.237). Thus physical abuse can be seen as an extension of the right to control and inculcate moral values, and the sexual abuse of female children an extension of the right of the male parent to have his sexual needs met.

The legal system is a reflection of the powerful patriarchal system of relationships within British society and finds exaggerations of that patriarchal system hard to deal with: 'Law defines the character and creates the institutions and social relationships within which the family operates. The legal system is constantly recreating a particular ideological view of relationships between the sexes, best expressed as an ideology of patriarchalism' (Freeman 1984, p.55).

A crucial duality that affects child protection work within the legal system is the divide between the criminal and civil strands of the law. This division has not been substantially affected by the arrival of the Children Act 1989, which, in the main, is concerned with the civil law. This section gives a brief outline of how both parts of the legal process can affect child protection work.

The criminal law

Much child abuse involves the adult (perpetrator) breaking the criminal law by assaulting the child (victim). One way in which the legal system can help the child protection effort is by successfully prosecuting the perpetrator of that abuse. But in Britain, Ireland, and to a lesser extent the USA, the criminal law is not effective in prosecuting perpetrators of abuse. In Britain, few cases of abuse reach the stage of charging, and even less are accepted for full prosecution by the Crown Prosecution Service (CPS). For example, within the first year of the working of the *Memorandum of Good Practice* (Home Office/DoH 1992), where children's evidence was recorded in special interviews for use in criminal prosecution, less than 1 in 300 were accepted by the Crown Prosecution Service for use in court, and even less were actually used in successful prosecutions (Cohen 1993, p.9). Even when an adult is found guilty of quite a serious form of abuse, the sentence offered is often less severe than if the assault had been perpetrated against an adult.

Practice scenario 7.2

Mr Larkin had killed his infant son in quite a brutal way and had tried to dispose of the body. In court, the charge was reduced to manslaughter.

> He was sentenced to three years' imprisonment and served less than two. In his home town, the ACPC had not yet finished working out the changes that the death suggested for the system, and the practitioners in his local area had hardly recovered from the experience, when they discovered that Mr Larkin was already back in their local community.

The process of child protection and criminal law

In child protection cases, the criminal legal process goes through several distinct stages. At each stage the process may be halted because of lack of proof or corroborative evidence, or because the case has not been or is not likely to be proven. The stages are as follows:

1   The assault/abusive behaviour occurs.
2   The assault/abusive behaviour is reported by the victim or a professional or lay observer.
3   Police and Social Services mount an investigation.
4   If sufficient evidence is available, the Police will charge the perpetrator and forward the file to the CPS.
5   The CPS considers the file, the likelihood of successful prosecution and the public interest. The charges will either be dropped or a court case will be organised.
6   The case goes to court.
7   The judge, jury or magistrate's bench will decide if the case has been proven beyond reasonable doubt and, if a guilty verdict is arrived at, will decide on an appropriate sentence.

In the case of child sexual abuse the current rate of successful prosecution is very low. The reasons for this low correlation between reported abuse and successful prosecution lie in the law and in its relationship with abused children and with all young people. They include:

- Physical, forensic evidence of abuse is often not present (or is easy to cast doubt on).
- Before the age of approximately 12 years the court will seldom accept direct evidence from children. Even after this age, a child or young person's evidence will normally be given less credibility than that of an adult witness: 'Up to now the qualitative difference between adult and child communication is in the legal system taken as merely a quantitative difference, with the result

that in cases of conflict children lie and adults speak the truth' (Furniss 1991, p.6).

- The British adversarial system, unaffected by the Children Act 1989, allows the no-holds-barred cross-examination of children. Children and young people, particularly those who have been abused, will experience that cross-examination as bullying, and may quickly 'cave in' under that pressure, experiencing it as being abusive: 'the legal rules that govern the evidence of children create serious problems for the courts in doing justice where children are the victims of violence or sexual abuse. They cause difficulties in criminal as well as in civil cases: but in criminal cases the law is at its worst' (Spencer and Flin 1990, p.327).

Practice scenario 7.3

Mary was 14 and was giving evidence at the trial of her maternal uncle whom she claimed had been sexually abusing her over a period of three years. Mary answered the prosecuting barrister in a nervous but quite clear fashion. When it came to the defending barrister's cross-examination, he asked three questions in an accusatory and belligerent manner, clearly seeking to undermine Mary's credibility as a witness.

The first question was: did Mary know what the truth was?

Mary replied yes.

The second question was: did Mary read the Bible?

Mary was silent.

The third question (repeated twice) was: did Mary know her scriptures?

At which point Mary dissolved into tears.

Mary was a child from a non-religious family. The second question had confused her, the third she had not understood at all, but she had clearly understood that this respectable, powerful, adult male was calling her a liar. The case against her uncle fell.

- Last, and perhaps most important, the criminal system requires that guilt be established 'beyond reasonable doubt' before a successful prosecution can be made. Because child abuse occurs behind closed doors, because a child's evidence is given less credence than the adult's, and because the patriarchal court system sometimes tries to give the benefit of the doubt to male perpetrators, proving a child abuse case in criminal court can be extremely difficult.

In Britain in the early 1990s the Home Office and Department of Health prepared several publications that aimed to help in this matter. The *Memorandum of Good Practice* (Home Office/DoH 1992) proposed a code of acceptable interview procedures for joint investigation of child sexual abuse and the *Child Witness Pack* (Plotnikoff 1993) gave advice on how best to prepare children for their courtroom ordeal.

The government ministers responsible (M. Jack and T. Yeo) admitted that there existed a problem with regard to children and the criminal court: 'All too often the interests of justice have been frustrated – and the child further harmed by the legal process' (Home Office/DoH 1992, Foreword), but claimed that the advice or guidance offered within the booklets would be able to change those problems: 'you the practitioner will be able to make the guidance work for children and for justice'.

It seems that, instead of changing the law to fit the reality of child abuse, child protection practitioners and children themselves were to be encouraged to 'squeeze' their reality into a form more palatable to the court.

The civil law

The civil law is substantially different to the criminal law in that it does not try to establish guilt, but investigates the competing claims for social or financial disposals between two or more people. It is the civil law which includes all emergency, care and matrimonial proceedings concerning children. With civil law, the balance of proof is very different from the criminal law, in that the court must establish under a balance of probabilities what has occurred and that a decision is correct.

The process

Matrimonial or divorce proceedings are called 'private law applications', and seldom include child abuse matters. These applications vastly outnumber public law applications (largely care proceedings) under the Children Act 1989. Care proceedings, under the civil law, can be a complex process which may be terminated at any stage, if the reason for taking out the proceedings becomes invalid. The Children Act 1989 also holds a key 'no order concept' that attempts to obviate all unnecessary litigation and child care orders. Although the process can vary from case to case, a typical path for a public law care application might be (see Figure 2.3):

1 A case of physical abuse is referred through to the duty officer in Social Services.
2 Two field social workers organise the investigation with the help of their senior and of the consultant paediatrician.
3 If the injury is severe and probably not accidental, the child may indicate that it is the responsibility of the caretaker, who may act in an aggressive, uncooperative way.
4 The social worker or team leader rings the local Magistrate's Court clerk, who organises a special *ex parte* hearing in front of a magistrate.
5 The magistrate grants/refuses to grant an Emergency Protection Order (EPO). This order lasts for up to eight days, authorising the removal of the child from the abusive situation into a non-abusive situation (often from family to local authority care).
6 Between the EPO and the full care hearing a number of other processes are going on simultaneously:

   • The social worker has the duty to investigate the possibility of early rehabilitation at home or the placement of the child with relatives. She also has to formulate a partnership of work with the family which attempts to bring them into the process to achieve positive change.
   • The parents have the right, after 72 hours have elapsed, to challenge the orders, often doing so at a series of interim care hearings held in the Magistrate's Court. Those same hearings will be responsible for reviewing issues of contact between child and family.
   • A series of directions hearings will take place with solicitors representing all parties, the clerk and the social worker or team leader. These hearings attempt to sort out in advance the issues which might be contentious in the full hearing.
   • The guardian ad litem will be preparing her report.
   • All parties will be preparing and submitting their evidence for full disclosure before the full hearing.

7 At the full hearing, the issues that are in dispute are aired by solicitors acting for all parties – often local authority, parents and guardian ad litem. All have a right to present their evidence and to cross-examine the witnesses. The professionals involved in the case from the multi-disciplinary network may be called as witnesses to the full hearing.

8   At the end of the hearing the magistrates will decide whether to grant a Care Order, a Supervision Order, another order, or to grant no order at all.
9   Parents have the right to appeal against the decision to a higher court. The child protection system then has a duty to explore the area of positive change and rehabilitation. If no change is achieved the court can again be approached to free the child for permanent adoptive placement.

Having discussed some of the crucial areas of child protection law and process, it would be appropriate to examine some of the key players who staff that legal process. Although all child protection practitioners and managers could potentially participate in the legal intervention, there are certain practitioner groups who are key, permanent participants in the court process.

The judge

Role

Despite hearing relatively few child protection cases (particularly since the reduction of wardship cases in the early 1990s) the judge, sitting in the family division of High Court, the Care Centre, the Family Hearing Centre and the County Court, holds a key role with regard to childcare law. He or she will make legal decisions about the most difficult of child protection cases that have been referred from the lower court. He or she will also sit on appeal hearings on disputed cases from the Magistrate's Court. Thus the translation of the law and the making of case law are often the domain of the judge. This role is particularly important following the enactment of significant pieces of childcare legislation such as the Children Act 1989.

Qualification

The judge or recorder are qualified barristers who, through experience and recommendation, have been promoted into the judiciary.

Training

The judge will be trained in the law, trained to present a case and trained to weigh the merits of a legal submission. Specific training in childcare and child abuse matters was limited until the Lord Chancellor's Department encouraged a minimum programme of training to equip the judiciary to work with the new Children Act 1989. However, training alongside other (non-legal) practitioner groups is rare.

Areas of interest and concern

A

One general area of concern is that the judiciary do not represent the population at large; that, in the main, they are older, white, middle-class males. In terms of child protection that could mean that they would find it difficult to appreciate the reality of the experience of an abused child and that they would find it much easier to appreciate the perspective of the adult males involved. This having been said, it would be appropriate to point out that some of the most child-centred, pioneering work in the legal sphere (particularly with regard to the Children Act 1989) has been undertaken by senior women judges in the family division of the High Court.

B

Their training, primarily within the law – a law that finds it difficult to deal with child abuse – is not the most appropriate background for the very difficult decisions that must be made about the future familial care of children:

> in looking to the future the court has to assess the risk. The court should not be asked to perform in every case a strict legalistic analysis ... The words of the statute must be considered but parliament did not intend them to be unduly restrictive when the evidence clearly indicated that a certain course should be taken in order to protect the child. (*Newham LBC* v. *AG* [1993] 1 FLR 281; [1993] FL 122(CA))

What is certain is that the Children Act 1989 has exaggerated a process that began with the increased use of wardship legislation in the 1980s. It has moved the judiciary and magistracy further away from their area of expertise (the law) and towards a responsibility for detailed decisions that concern childcare, child development, child abuse and family life. These decisions were formerly the exclusive areas of expertise of the child welfare agencies; the judiciary are poorly prepared and trained to move into this new practice domain.

The magistrate

If the judge is the experienced legal professional, then the magistrate is the experienced amateur of the legal system. Nevertheless, the magistrate's role is crucial to that legal intervention. The magistrate will process the vast majority of public and private childcare applications in England and Wales. The Children Act 1989 has combined many of the functions of the old juvenile and civil courts into the one Family Proceedings Court, leaving those magistrates who sit within that court an increasingly complex work task.

Role

The Magistrate's Court, with its members sitting as part of their Children's Panel in the Family Proceedings Court, will process the majority of child protection work that comes through the courts in England and Wales (only 15–25 per cent of cases will go to a higher court). Cases are only transferred to the higher courts if the Magistrate's Court considers it to be appropriate. This transfer will only be on grounds of the length, complexity or difficulty of the expected proceedings. Therefore most applications for Emergency Protection Orders, Child Assessment Orders, Care and Supervision Orders will be heard in front of a bench of magistrates in the Family Proceedings Court.

Qualification

Few magistrates (apart from stipendiary or professional magistrates) will have specific legal training because, in terms of the law, the magistrate works as an amateur, giving judgment that reflects the community and its values. However, many magistrates will hold many different qualifications from other walks of life, sometimes qualifications concerned with working with children.

Training

In order to become a magistrate the candidate will have had to undergo a brief introduction to the legal process. Some magistrates will then elect to go onto the Children's or Family Panels to hear public and private law cases that concern children. These magistrates will receive some training on child protection and the Children Act 1989: 'they must receive the required specialist training and have experience in dealing with family matters before they can be nominated to sit' (CAAC

1992, p.10). This training will probably be organised on a single-disciplinary basis. Within court, less experienced magistrates will always be paired with an experienced chairperson, and so may learn and train in this way.

Areas of interest and concern

A

The increased role and power of the magistrate will not necessarily lead to better child protection decisions being made. The limited experience and training in child protection for some magistrates may lead to some difficulty in making very complex childcare decisions.

B

Although the magistrate's bench is supposed to reflect the community, there is frequently some difficulty in getting the make-up of the bench to reflect the population of the community at large. For example, in communities with large black populations there are often few black magistrates. Children and young people are never represented on the bench.

C

The role and power of the magistrate when compared to an experienced court clerk can be seen to be diminished, particularly in an area as controversial as child abuse (see below).

D

On the other hand, it is clear that Family Proceedings Courts are staffed by magistrates who are highly motivated to make the best decisions for children. This, allied with the fact that the Magistrate's Court bench does, to some extent, represent the community, could make the magistrate a positive resource for the child protection system.

The court clerk

The clerk is the facilitator of the Magistrate's Court process. He or she forms a partnership with the magistrate that is in itself a multi-disciplinary relationship – the amateur magistrate as decision-maker combined with the professional legal adviser as facilitator of the process.

Role

The clerk's role is to act as an adviser, legal expert and administrator to the magistrates when they are making a decision. The clerk, during emergency and care proceedings, will organise and orchestrate directions hearings which control legal activity before the stage of court appearance. Whilst actually in court the clerk will occupy the same role of adviser and facilitator. Although the clerk is actually appointed and supervised by the local magistrate's bench, in the mid-1990s the Home Office has made moves towards a more centralised form of control.

Qualification

It is increasingly common that the court clerk will have qualified as a solicitor or barrister, as well as having the more specific clerks' training.

Training

Clerks will often receive little child protection training, usually not on a multi-disciplinary basis.

Areas of interest and concern

A

Although the court clerk is present to advise the magistrates, because of their expert status and their control of the administrative machinery their power can be considerable, particularly with regard to a less experienced or assertive bench.

The barrister

Up to the 1980s the involvement of barristers within the child protection legal process was small. This area of work was not particularly lucrative and few cases went beyond the level of the Magistrate's Court. At this time there was a rapid expansion of the use of wardship proceedings in the High Court. This opened up this area of work to a small number of barristers. The Family Law Bar Association seeks to represent and to inform that particular group of barristers.

Role

The barrister's role is to present the case of the local authority, the parents, the child, the guardian ad litem or any other party to proceedings in the County or High Court. Another traditional role for senior barristers (Queen's Counsels) is to chair independent reviews or inquiries into child deaths or serious mishaps in individual child protection systems. Senior barristers may also move on into the judiciary, where some will continue to work in the child law field.

Training

Apart from an amount of introductory training on the Children Act 1989, most barristers will receive little specific child protection training; instead they will gain their knowledge from actual work within court.

Areas of interest and concern

A

Because the barrister only sees the legal translation of child protection work within the court setting, they lack an appreciation of the social, emotional and psychological trauma that child abuse can hold for the child. This can result in barristers experiencing difficulties in understanding and translating the reality of child abuse or family life to the court.

B

As with judges and recorders, barristers are primarily white, male and middle-class. This can be an extra barrier to appreciating child abuse, particularly when this abuse involves an abuse of patriarchal power.

The solicitor

The solicitor is the practitioner who represents the parties to care proceedings in the lower (primarily Magistrate's) courts, and instructs the barrister on behalf of the client in the higher courts. The local authority is frequently represented by solicitors from their own legal department; other parties are usually represented by solicitors in private practice.

The local authority solicitor is increasingly involved in case conferences as a giver of legal advice and is heavily involved in the early stages of the child protection process in applying for Emergency Protection, Child Assessment, or Interim Care Orders.

The Law Society's Children's Panel involves a number of solicitors whose experience in childcare matters leads to a particular skill in that area; the Family Law Association is a professional association of solicitors that represents those working in this specialist area.

Qualification

Some solicitors will have law degrees, but all will have completed their 'articles' – a mixture of practical apprenticeship and theoretical examination. Child protection would not usually form a part of this experience.

Training

The Children Act 1989 brought a considerable amount of preparatory training to some solicitors. However, it would be unusual for solicitors to have had a considerable amount of child protection training, and most unusual for this to have taken place in a multi-disciplinary setting. Before being included in the Children's Panel a solicitor will have been expected to undertake two days' training in child law and child protection issues. But, in the main, solicitors gain their knowledge through practical court experience.

Areas of interest and concern

A

As with barristers and judges, solicitors only gain their child protection experience through court work. Their wider knowledge and understanding of the child's experience and the roles and perspectives of other agencies is limited.

B

If the solicitor never experiences direct child contact, it is difficult for these professionals to be able to truly appreciate and represent the child's perspective to the court.

The Police

At the early stages of the organisation of child protection work in the 1970s there was some controversy about the inclusion of the Police Service in the protection system. This led, in some areas, to the Police not being involved in case conferences and not being informed about some cases of abuse. This situation has now been resolved with the full inclusion of the Police within the child protection process, and within the machinery of the ACPC.

Role

The Police are the investigatory arm of the criminal law. Their role within child protection is primarily to investigate if the criminal law has been broken, and to prepare evidential reports to be used in criminal proceedings. However, the Police also share a mutual protective responsibility that goes beyond the prosecuting of criminals: 'The success of the police intervention, however, is not to be measured in terms of the prosecutions which are brought, but of the protection which their actions bring to children at risk' (Home Office 1988, p.10).

Hallett and Birchall (1992) claim that the Police have increasingly subsumed their particular interests in favour of the child and wider whole: 'police have increasingly exercised their discretion and subordinated law-enforcement to the pursuit of the case conference's view of the child's best interests' (p.134). The Police's investigatory role is particularly relevant in cases of serious child physical abuse and in all cases of child sexual abuse. With sexual abuse, specially trained police and social workers will join together to undertake investigatory (memorandum) interviews with children to establish if enough evidence of sexual abuse can be gathered to justify prosecution of the alleged abuser.

The Police have also developed lesser roles that are concerned with civil law and the protection system. The first is that they are able to inform the child protection system if an adult is a 'Schedule 1' offender or not (that is, if an adult has a record of serious crimes against children). The second is that they are empowered to help social workers enforce orders under the civil law (for example, Emergency Protection Orders).

It is also the case that the Police, in many areas, have become active members of the local ACPCs, heavily involved in decision-making about general child protection policies in the local area.

Qualification

A probationary police officer will be in training for a period of two years. This period will include considerable practical experience and periods of non-practical theory and training. The particular issues involved in child protection may not feature highly in this process.

Training

After passing out as fully-fledged police officers, some police officers will undertake specialist training in the area of family violence and abuse. Some of this training will be of a multi-disciplinary nature – for example, the 'memorandum' training – and some will be of a single-disciplinary nature.

Areas of interest and concern

A

Although the Police are the main investigative arm of the criminal law, they do not exercise a great deal of power once that investigation is completed. Therefore, many possible prosecutions for child abuse matters are rejected by the Crown Prosecution Service without the Police exercising any control over their decisions.

B

There is a general gender and race bias within the Police Service towards white, male officers. It is significant, however, that, although women are in a minority within the service as a whole, they will form the majority of staff who undertake specialist family violence work – though the higher management of the Police child protection process remains a male domain.

C

Child protection work is not set apart, in the eyes of the public, from other areas of work, so a generally unsatisfactory relationship with some communities can be reflected in how children and adults react to the officers who are undertaking their child protection task. This was graphically shown in an excerpt from a monograph about how children see the members of different child protection agencies. Rashid (aged ten), an Asian child, commented on the difference between police and social workers: 'Police take people and hit them, social workers don't' (Barford 1993, p.30).

D

In recent years there has been a positive development in the gradual establishment of specialist teams within the Police Service to deal with child abuse or family violence in general. These teams have amassed a substantial amount of expertise that benefits the whole system.

E

A most important area of difference with regard to the Police Service is that their aim must primarily be that of the potential prosecution of an offender (the legal intervention). Although this perspective can cooperate successfully with the therapeutic and protection perspectives, if it attempts to take over it can have a damaging effect on the child and family: 'The specific nature of child sexual abuse ... makes it imperative that police and courts do not only consider how to intervene from their own perspective' (Furniss 1991, p.99).

F

Many authors have commented upon the potential for conflict between the field social worker and the police officer: 'the issues between police and social workers may be the most fraught because of the exceptional ambiguities and conflicts of care and control within their role and between their agencies' (Hallett and Birchall 1992, p.133).

Thomas (1994) comments upon the potential for conflict between what appear to be two diametrically opposed perspectives:

> The welfare–punishment dichotomy is quite apparent to the police who wish to arrest and charge, and to social workers who wish to preserve a family unit and to protect a child in other ways. The potential for conflict

is inherent in the availability of criminal prosecution and civil remedies, in ideologies of welfare and justice held up by either side. (p.80)

But this potential for conflict can be exaggerated, and the potential for each service not to appreciate the perspective of the other is prone to overstatement. As the report of the Bexley Project (Metropolitan Police/ London Borough of Bexley 1987) indicates:

> There was, from the outset, a question as to whether police officers and social workers would be able to work together in a spirit of mutual trust, without compromising their respective statutory and professional responsibilities. However, the agreed procedures developed for the project reflect each organisation's acceptance and acknowledgement of each other's statutory obligations, responsibilities and policies. This was usually achieved by some compromise being made on both sides. (p.7)

Peace (1991) went one step further, suggesting that there had been an improvement in relationships across the board:

> comments about the police and social work relationship were largely complimentary. Clearly this had not always been the case. Many said that there had been a marked improvement recently and often this was put down to conscious efforts made at a senior level by both agencies to talk and plan for better communication. (p.142)

The Memorandum of Good Practice (Home Office/DoH 1992) has put yet more demands on the co-working relationship of the police officer and social worker in the investigation of child sexual abuse, and has highlighted the potential strain between the protective and legal interventions. However, the probability of being able to work effectively, given positive inter-agency relationships, remains high.

The above are practitioners with a strictly legal background, with their roots and perspectives firmly grounded in the law. However, the legal system does employ some staff with a specifically welfare or social work orientation. These staff hold positions of some importance with regard to the child protection process.

The probation officer

The Probation Service is provided by the Home Office as an agency that not only serves the legal system, but attempts to represent the best interests of the alleged offender and their family within the legal process.

Role

Within child physical abuse and neglect, the probation officer holds the same role as any practitioner with professional contact with adults and families – that is, to be observant of parent–child interactions and to refer and discuss possible cases of abuse with the rest of the child protection network. It is in the area of child sexual abuse that the probation officer has a specialised part to play. The Probation Service has always worked with non-familial sex offenders. With the 're-discovery' of child sexual abuse in the 1980s, the service became heavily involved with community treatment programmes for familial offenders. This included the traditional work with perpetrators on their own, but also covered many new (sometimes multi-disciplinary) groupwork projects for perpetrators of child sexual abuse.

The Probation Service also offers a more general service to the civil legal system through its series of civil unit teams. These teams advise the court system on child and family matters during contested or disputed court proceedings, particularly around divorce. The welfare officer's role has increased under the Children Act legislation (CAAC 1992).

Qualification

All probation officers are qualified with the relevant social work qualification (CQSW or DipSW), but will have completed a specialist 'probation option' within that course. The Home Office sponsors their trainees on these courses, often choosing to sponsor probation volunteers who have worked as voluntary helpers in probation teams. The amount and quality of child protection training on DipSW courses will vary considerably (see 'The field social worker', Chapter 4).

Training

Probation officers will receive some training both in general child abuse work and in more specialised working with perpetrators of child sexual abuse. The quantity and quality of this training will vary between probation areas: sometimes this training will be offered on a multi-disciplinary basis.

Areas of concern

A

The Probation Service, as much as any other agency, understands how to combine the legal and the therapeutic interventions within child protection. However, because they are primarily an adult-based service, it is difficult for them to keep the needs of the child in focus.

Practice scenario 7.4

Mr Saxby was an experienced probation officer and had been working with James Hearn since he had been placed on a two-year Probation Order for extensive sexual abuse of his stepdaughter. During the first three months of the order Mr Saxby was impressed with his client's general demeanour, his contrition and his loving attitude towards his family. He called a multi-disciplinary meeting to discuss the eventual objective of his client returning home. During this meeting several other practitioners were able to put the child's perspective on James's relationship with his family. This changed the tone of the meeting entirely. Instead of a discussion of rehabilitation at home, the possibility of referring James to a perpetrators' group was discussed.

The guardian ad litem

The guardian ad litem will always be a qualified social worker who has considerable experience in childcare work. Although sometimes in the employ of the local authority and sometimes belonging to a voluntary social work organisation, they all act as independent advisers to the court on the needs and best interest of the child.

Role

The role of the guardian ad litem went through a rapid expansion in the early 1990s, with the increased perception of the need for separate representation of the child's interests. The guardian is now brought into the child protection process at an early stage (often at the first or second interim hearing), and will act in all care cases where there is the possibility of a difference of interest between the child and the other parties: 'A guardian ad litem must be appointed unless the court is satisfied that it is not necessary to do so in order to safeguard the child's interests' (CAAC 1992, p.13).

The guardian ad litem has a duty to represent the child's views to the court and to present their view of the child's best interest in the current situation. Where there is a possibility of difference between the child and the guardian ad litem, both can be separately represented in court.

In effect, the guardian ad litem examines and comments upon the seriousness of the original abuse, the child's relationship with her family, the possibility of safe rehabilitation and the plans of the local authority and child protection system:

> The role of the guardian ad litem is a complex one involving the utilisation of a range of skills as well as a thorough knowledge of social work theory and child care law ... The intention is to ensure that, through the guardian ad litem, the court is fully informed of the relevant facts which relate to the child's welfare and that the wishes and feelings of the child are clearly established. (CAAC 1992, p.14)

The guardian ad litem does not have the statutory power of the local authority or the court. However, because of their independent status and experience, the court and the legal system must take what they say seriously. They therefore wield considerable power in the child protection process, once that process has reached the stage of the legal intervention.

Qualification

Guardians ad litem will always be qualified social workers (CQSW or DipSW) who have undertaken extra training for their role. There is no formal extra qualification for the role.

Training

The guardian ad litem will have received the training in child protection that the average field social worker receives (see Chapter 4). They will also have undertaken extra training on the role of the guardian ad litem, which will include a more detailed study of the law and the legal system.

Areas of concern

A   Independence

The guardian ad litem is independent of all parties in a childcare case. However, because the guardian is a field social worker, often a local authority social worker, that independence has frequently been questioned: 'It is essential that the court and the public should have confidence in the independence of guardians and that guardians themselves should feel confident of their independent status' (Lyon and de Cruz 1993, p.378). In practice, however, the guardian ad litem and the field social worker do not often show this complicity or collusion. In fact, they frequently express differences of opinion or judgment about the case in question, and the guardian ad litem also feels very able to critically examine the field social worker's professional actions.

One disadvantage of this independence is that it is difficult to question or to appeal against the guardian ad litem's recommendations, because of their power and influence in court.

B   Support and supervision

Another disadvantage of this independent role is that the guardian ad litem could lack the normal support and supervision that fieldworkers would get from their colleagues and managers. The role and position of the guardian ad litem can be even more stressful than the field social worker, because of the difficulty of sharing the stresses and strains of the work. All guardians ad litem in England and Wales belong to one of 56 'panels'. Support and supervision are established at the discretion of the individual panel.

Conclusion

The Children Act 1989 brought substantial change to how child protection cases were processed through the legal system in England and Wales. The renewal and simplification of childcare law, the lessening of divisions between the different court organisations, the increased use of the guardian ad litem and the emphasis on the need to train relevant legal practitioners were all significant and positive changes. These improvements were matched with a considerable commitment on the part of key legal professionals to make the Act work in practice. Despite their considerable effort, however, the Children Act 1989 has failed to challenge many of the factors in the English and Welsh legal system that block effective child protection work. These factors include:

- The lack of a Family Court. Childcare issues, although recognised as particular and special, must nevertheless be included and fitted in to the normal adult-orientated court system.
- The legal process still retains the adversarial system in spite of the indications that an inquisitorial system (as in the Scottish Children's Panel or French *Juge des Enfants*) offers a more flexible way of discovering a child's needs.
- The legal system in England and Wales retains a heavily patriarchal flavour which, as we have already seen, is not wholly appropriate in child protection matters, particularly when working with the child's right to be free from abuse: 'judicial paternalism has been perceived as curbing the growth of children's so-called "rights", and forcing commentators to re-evaluate, in the context of the 1989 Act, whether such "rights" really exist' (Lyon and de Cruz 1993, p.379).
- Because of all of the above, the legal system finds it difficult to truly hear and process the contribution of the child or those that work closely with that child. In some cases (most notably within child sexual abuse and the criminal law), the child's contribution is positively discouraged and disallowed.

It is certainly true to say that the court and the practitioners around it must retain their independence of action. However, the court must also allow this independence to practitioners who belong to other interventions:

> No other professional can tell the police, public prosecutors or courts how to deal legally with cases of child sexual abuse ... The specific nature of child sexual abuse ... however, makes it imperative that police and courts do not only consider how to intervene from their own perspective. (Furniss 1991, p.99)

In some ways the court arena has become the place where the different interventions meet and collide: 'The conflicts of professional and agency orientation are particularly acute at the legal interface, where detection, justice, protection and therapy all attempt to meet' (Hallett and Birchall 1992, p.199). With the increasing power of the court system, there is the possibility that that system becomes more and more involved in all aspects of child protection work.

Although it is appropriate for the court to be the arbiter in particularly contentious issues, the justification for this role is not that the court has any expertise in childcare or child abuse, but that its independence from any of the involved parties can be relied upon. As an organisation that is primarily concerned with what is, and is not, legal, with what can, or cannot, be proved, it should not be over-involved in either the social interactions within families, or the therapeutic interaction between the professional system and its clients.

8   Voluntary organisations

Although voluntary social work organisations do not now seem as influential and powerful as the larger, statutory ACPC agencies, their contribution and their role within the child protection process has been crucial to the development of that process, and is still very important in its enactment. Many of the larger voluntary organisations, including Barnardo's, National Children's Homes (NCH), The Children's Society, the National Children's Bureau and the Family Welfare Association, were set up in the Victorian era in response to the growing concern about the children of the urban poor, and the awareness that the existing Poor Law provision did not encompass the special needs of these children. All of these organisations still retain a wide childcare brief, of which child protection is a part. The NSPCC, however, although established in the same era (it was founded in 1884), began and maintained a very specialist child abuse focus.

In the 1980s, over a hundred years after the establishment of these voluntary organisations, another wave of smaller voluntary organisations and pressure groups came into being. These were specifically orientated towards different aspects of childcare and child abuse. Among these, the Family Rights Group (FRG), National Association for Young People in Care (NAYPIC), the Children's Legal Centre and Childline were very significant.

At a regional level, there exists a plethora of voluntary organisations that either subscribe to a national scheme – for example, Home-start, Victim Support or Newpin – or exist with a purely local orientation. These voluntary organisations all hold charitable status and are funded, in different degrees, by a mixture of public donation and local authority funding. Funding from central government is limited.

At the beginning of the 1980s, the belief that voluntary organisations might replace the local authority in many areas of childcare provision was an ideologically attractive prospect to many in the Conservative Party. This change has not occurred. In fact, the 1990s, because of the recession and reduction of local authority funding, has seen the wholesale reorganisation and reduction in the amount and breadth of voluntary organisation work. Some, in fact (Childline and NAYPIC most notably), have struggled even to survive.

In the Victorian era the voluntary organisations formed a partnership with the local authority, leaving the authority with the smaller, residual role. In the modern era, however, this partnership has, to a large extent, been reversed. The big, statutory ACPC agencies undertake the bulk of child protection work, with the voluntary organisations undertaking the smaller, more specialised, developmental roles.

This balance of involvement, this partnership of childcare provision, is reflected in other European countries, where voluntary, sometimes religious, social work organisations share responsibility for childcare and child protection with the statutory sector.

The NSPCC

The NSPCC has played a crucial role in the development of child protection work for over a century. The organisation has maintained a strong profile in terms of the political and public appreciation of abuse, with an emphasis on the ability to influence public opinion and policy-makers at the highest level. Their specialist focus, allied with their ability to influence the public appreciation of abuse, has made them influential in the drafting of important pieces of childcare legislation (for example, the Children Acts of both 1889 and 1989). In return for their assistance in the drafting of legislation, that same legislation consistently confirmed the NSPCC's special statutory rights to independent action in the child protection field (even though, in the 1990s, these rights are seldom used).

Social work organisation

The NSPCC has maintained a national network of field social work staff since the 1880s. For the first eighty years of its existence this network underwent very little change. It consisted of individual inspectors or small teams, trained by the NSPCC themselves, who worked in geographical 'patches', responding to all reports of child neglect or cruelty in their area.

The Children Act 1948 heralded the establishment of a specialist, professionalised local authority childcare service in the Children's Departments. These departments were gradually to undertake a greater share of the protective work of the NSPCC. Thus, by the 1960s, the NSPCC's inspectorate staff offered quite a generalised child welfare service, far removed from their early developmental role in child abuse.

The 're-discovery' of physical abuse in the USA offered an opportunity to the NSPCC to regain their pioneering role. They set up the Denver House action research project in London in 1968. This project introduced into the British system the new knowledge about child physical abuse that had been developed by the Kempes in the USA. Denver House was to pioneer a radical change in the work and organisation of the NSPCC in England and Wales. Not only did it re-focus the society's work right back into the centre of child abuse, but also it began a movement away from a universal provision of an inspectorate service, towards a more focused provision based on specialist teams. The next specialist team was set up in Manchester in 1973 and the society's centenary appeal in 1984 funded the complete reorganisation of the society's social work division into 66 specialist child protection teams.

When these teams were first established in the 1970s, they often undertook central organisational tasks on behalf of the ACPC, particularly the running of the central Child Protection Register and the chairing of case conferences. These central tasks were often onerous, purely concerned with the protective intervention, sometimes preventing the teams who undertook them from fully developing their therapeutic role (Pickett 1990). The late 1980s saw a considerable rise in the provision of specialist teams by Social Services Departments, and the withdrawing of the NSPCC from their central role with regard to Child Protection Registers. The period of the late 1980s and 1990s has been one in which the NSPCC has attempted to discover a new role for itself. The fundamental review of 1991 seemed to suggest a flexibility that would allow individual area teams to fill the gaps in local child protection provision. However, this local flexibility lacks a unity and consistency of development and purpose.

Role

Within the NSPCC's 66 child protection units there is much variation in role; however, there are clear patterns to the different teams' work programmes. In general, there seems to be a move away from the protective intervention towards the preventative and therapeutic interventions. Therefore the NSPCC has largely withdrawn from the investigative stages of abuse work and from their role as coordinators of registers and case conferences. Instead, the teams are concentrating most of their effort in the area of prevention and post-conference assessment and therapeutic work. Some teams are also developing expertise in training, and many will participate fully in the organisation of their local ACPCs.

At a national level, the society set up an inquiry in 1994 to attempt to discover and review the strengths and the ongoing weaknesses of the British child protection system; this move clearly indicates the society's intention to remain at the centre of the national debate about child protection policy and practice.

Qualification

The NSPCC fieldwork staff are primarily qualified social workers (CQSW or DipSW), some with many years' post-qualification experience.

Training

As well as the input from their qualification course, the NSPCC fieldwork staff will undergo induction training and will have the opportunity to participate in substantial amounts of specialised child protection training, often organised within the NSPCC itself. Some NSPCC teams will also facilitate substantial amounts of training for other practitioners in the multi-disciplinary system.

Areas of interest and concern

A

The NSPCC contains some of the most experienced, often well-supervised, child protection managers and practitioners. Sometimes these talents are under-used within the child protection systems they serve.

B

Because the role of the NSPCC is very closely related to that of the field social worker, there is a constant struggle to avoid duplication. As the Maria Colwell Inquiry (DHSS 1974) pointed out: 'If the NSPCC is considering a long-term shift of emphasis it might be to the benefit of children at risk both by the avoidance of duplication and by the development of specialised treatment and research' (p.71).

C

This possible duplication of role can sometimes lead to uneasy relationships with Social Services Departments. Peace (1991) quotes from the interview of a Director of Social Services: 'When NSPCC ... first arrived there was some feeling throughout the social services departments that they were an imposition. The feeling was "get lost, we'll do our own thing". They have a role on the Area Review Committee to give advice, and we didn't particularly welcome that either' (p.137).

This view contrasts with the positive experience of actually sharing work with the NSPCC that many practitioners from the multi-disciplinary system report. It seems that the specialist input of the NSPCC will either be welcomed or rejected, depending largely on the relationship between the NSPCC team and their local system.

D

Although the NSPCC teams can affect child protection work directly, they can also influence child protection practice in general by their consultancy, training and exposition of new ways of working. This influence is considerable, but is only effective if the particular system concerned is open to such an influence.

Practice scenario 8.1

The Milltown NSPCC child protection team had been in existence for over twelve years. The team had developed new ways of working with abuse that they outlined through training and written material. This work had had an influence at a national level, and had had considerable impact on the staff in some neighbouring ACPCs. However, because of strong antipathy by local social work practitioners and managers, the model was never fully taken on board within their home area.

E

The true strength of the NSPCC (which is shared by other voluntary organisations) is that it is not restricted purely by statutory duties and can develop flexible ways of working to deal with different aspects of abuse. It is in this developmental role that the NSPCC can best utilise their fieldwork service. Although there have been times in its history when it has been clear what that developmental role should be, unfortunately such a clarity is lacking at the turn of the twentieth century.

F

As with most large voluntary organisations, the substantial social work division of the NSPCC is shadowed by a large fundraising division (the NSPCC is largely financed through public donations). The financial appeals of the fundraising division have been based on perceptions of child abuse that have not substantially changed over the last century. So, although the fieldwork division has moved away from the crisis-led inspectorate service, the fundraising division has preferred to remain within the old paradigm. This dichotomy of social work action and charitable appeal is very marked.

The established child welfare voluntary organisations

There exist within the British system a number of well-established, large, voluntary organisations. They include the Children's Society, Barnardo's, National Children's Homes, Boys' and Girls' Welfare Society, Family Service Units and the National Children's Bureau. These are all long-established childcare organisations with a generalist concern with child welfare. Most of these societies operate from large, central headquarters, but do most of their work in small, local projects in different parts of the country. These projects will reflect the general ethos of the voluntary organisation and the perceived service need in the given locality. Some of these projects will be partially or wholly concerned with child abuse, as an Area Social Services Manager told Peace: 'We invite the voluntary sector to fill gaps ... We have some agreed priorities and point voluntaries in the direction of identified need ... on the other hand the voluntary agency's role should be assertive; they should be an alternative source of defining needs' (Peace 1991, p.138).

In terms of child protection work, these long-established voluntary organisations will establish, in consultation with statutory bodies and the ACPC, where the gaps are in local provision, and try to develop a service to fill them. In doing so, however, they still retain the right to separate definition of, and action on, the task that they have undertaken.

For example, the National Children's Homes, a long-established, Christian voluntary organisation, has developed, on behalf of local systems, a network of Family Centres that undertake a range of tasks including family assessments, supervision of contact and development of parenting skills. Although the voluntary organisation will supervise these centres itself, the work is done in conjunction with, and on behalf of, the local child protection system. Local projects are often partly or wholly financed by the local authority.

Specific voluntary organisations and pressure groups

Unlike the larger voluntary organisations with a general child welfare role, established long ago, there are a series of smaller voluntary organisations which were established partly or wholly as a reaction to the establishment of the modern child protection system. These organisations seek not only to offer a service to the particular constituency that they represent, but also to act as advocate, pressure group or legal adviser on their behalf. Child abuse frequently involves substantial differences of interest between those involved in the abusive interaction. These voluntary organisations reflect those differences and attempt to represent the needs of one particular group involved in that interaction.

The Family Rights Group and Parents Against Injustice

Although two distinct organisations, the FRG and PAIN are both aligned with the family welfare perspective in child abuse. Both seek to act as supporters of, and pressure groups on behalf of, the families (often parents) of children who are involved in the child protection process.

Role

As well as acting in individual cases and providing information on child protection procedure and law, the two organisations have become very effective in representing their view to policy-makers at all levels of government. Thus, from their response to the draft *Working Together* (FRG 1986) to their representation of parents before the Cleveland Inquiry, and their influential contribution to the consultation stages of the Children Act 1989, their influence and their ability to represent their perspective is not in doubt.

The National Association of Young People in Care and the Children's Legal Centre

NAYPIC was born in the late 1970s when the National Children's Homes brought together a number of children in care to express their views, as consumers, on the care that they received. The publication *Who Cares?* (NCH 1979) was produced some months later, and NAYPIC was formed shortly afterwards. The Children's Legal Centre was established in response to a similar perceived lack of representation of the child's legal interests.

Both organisations have espoused a strong child rights perspective, attempting to establish a minimum level of rights and an acceptable relationship between adult and child in the care, legal and child protection systems.

Role

The Children's Legal Centre acts as a monitor, pressure group and advocate in legal cases that concern children, and in the formation of new legislation that may concern children and young people. The centre's journal – *Childright* – is its means of dissemination of information and publicity. It has also published guides and information sheets on various aspects of the law.

NAYPIC's role is to attempt to represent the separate interests of children in care. This will be done on an individual basis, but NAYPIC will also act as a pressure group and advocate in particularly difficult cases. In recent years NAYPIC has taken on the role of combatting the most exaggerated forms of institutional abuse. This has involved a publicity campaign to expose institutional abuse, followed by quite forceful representation to the inquiries that are the result. NAYPIC's role in the Pindown Inquiry (Levy and Kahan 1991) in Staffordshire and the Beck Inquiry in Leicestershire has been crucial to the struggle against institutional abuse in residential care.

Areas of interest and concern

The financial and political vulnerability of these smaller voluntary organisations was ably illustrated in 1994 when NAYPIC, after several years of internal difficulties, ran out of money and effectively collapsed.

Childline

In 1986, following a prolonged campaign about child sexual abuse by the *That's Life* BBC television programme, the new telephone helpline Childline was established.

On their first evening of operation the response of children to the new service was slow, but since that time the demand for the Childline service has increased to such an extent that the majority of attempted telephone contacts cannot be answered.

Role

Childline unashamedly takes the needs and perspective of the child or young person as its starting point. It is a telephone counselling service which allows the child to define what she wants and what she feels is abusive. It is confidential in that it leaves control of the information with the child, and will not refer issues of abuse to child protection systems, unless the child herself specifically requests that this happens. However, Childline also gives children advice on how to get help and how to contact statutory agencies if they wish to.

Qualification and training

Childline staff will all have completed induction training in counselling, child abuse and Childline policy and procedure. Some staff will be undertaking more advanced counselling skills training.

Areas of interest and concern

A

Childline has succeeded in what it set out to do – it has established itself as a service for children in distress. Unfortunately, like NAYPIC, its success is no guarantee of its survival. At the same time as attempting to improve and expand its service to meet expressed demand, it has had a difficult task in remaining financially viable.

B

Because Childline espouses a children's rights perspective, which is not shared by most statutory agencies, the potential for conflict (particularly concerning areas of confidentiality and the right of the child to control her own contact with the helping agency) will always be a factor.

Local child- and parent-orientated organisations

At a local level, voluntary organisations have frequently been established which seek to help families with parenting issues (for example, Home-start and Newpin), or attempt to represent the interests of individual childcare workers or organisations (for example, local childminders or private nursery organisations). These organisations often have considerable helpful contact with children and families, and can be particularly active in helping to develop parenting skills, or help relieve the burden of parenting on families under stress. Their contact, training and perspective on the child protection process will vary according to area and the particular organisation. If involved in the process, these voluntary organisations often maintain a linking role between the family and child concerned and the statutory organisations that are working with them.

Adult-orientated voluntary organisations

There is a multiplicity of voluntary organisations which are concerned with adults and adult services – these include organisations for the elderly, for people with disabilities, learning difficulties, mental illness, and for people with specific illnesses and specific problems (for example, people with substance abuse problems or people who have been victims of crime). Adult-orientated counselling services are offered in many different settings. Some of these organisations work with adults who are also parents, and, because child abuse affects children from all walks of life, these adults and organisations will often be involved in the child protection arena.

The level of involvement and awareness within these organisations will vary greatly. As we have already noted, a strong adult orientation (see Chapter 7) may block the ability to focus on the child's separate needs.

Conclusion

Few voluntary organisations in Britain focus solely on child protection work. Because of the volume and complexity of the child protection task, it is difficult for small voluntary organisations to offer a wide-scale service to abused children and their families. The desire of the Conservative Right to devolve work from the statutory organisations to the voluntary sector in child protection terms has proved to be a chimera. However, voluntary organisations still play a key role in the British child protection scene. What they offer is an articulate and independent service which does not defer to government or the large, statutory organisations, but which can stimulate and develop the child protection service in particular local areas of need.

Part III

Working together

9 Child protection work and the individual

The last two parts have outlined and discussed the different organisational factors which shape and affect the multi-disciplinary child protection effort. In this chapter it is appropriate to engage in a discussion about the very real effects that the individual can have on that cooperative effort and the effects that that effort can have on the individual. In spite of agency, training and professional perspectives, there are some elements of cooperation or conflict that stem from the individual or the self, rather than the agency or practitioner group: 'The problems associated with personality clashes, whether perceived as related to a particular profession or an individual attitude, do not disappear because an organisational framework exists compelling professionals to work together' (Peace 1991, p.18).

The three subject areas that are discussed below are not exhaustive, but they are the areas that are most strongly connected with this personal dimension. They are:

- Personal history/personal reaction
- Areas of power and inequality
- The effects of stress.

Personal history/personal reaction

As well as bringing all our perspectives and baggage from our lives as practitioners, we also bring to our child protection work our personal histories of being a child, an adult and perhaps a parent. Child protection can cut across our feelings and experience in some of the most personal parts of our lives; those experiences and feelings can have a powerful effect on our professional behaviour. There is a myth, sub-scribed to by most professional groups involved in child protection work, which suggests that whilst at work one can leave the self or the personal part of the practitioner at home. However, no matter how 'professional' we try to be, those personal histories and feelings travel to work with us every day: 'Unless we work with our conflicts, con-fusions, disgusts and deep satisfactions they will skew our work. Nothing makes us so aware of our sexuality and anger as sexual abuse' (Moore 1992, p.60). Moore reminds us that this split between the professional and the personal is largely false, and the myth of the personal–professional 'split' is likely to reduce rather than increase our individual and collective effectiveness.

At one time it was hypothesised that strong personal reactions to protection work would be limited to those who had experienced severe abuse in childhood. The Rochdale NSPCC team took straw polls in the mid-1980s which suggested that a high proportion of those pro-fessionals who attended their training courses had been abused them-selves in childhood (the implication being that many child protection practitioners had experienced abuse). It was surmised that these prac-titioners were likely to experience severe reactions to abuse work that would substantially affect the quality of the service that they gave (Dale et al. 1986).

Our current understanding of personal history and personal reaction is more complicated than this. The severity of an individual's reaction is not just based on whether, or how badly, an individual has been abused. It is important to move away from the 'sheep or goats' (abused or not abused) way of understanding, towards a situation where we recognise that a multiplicity of personal factors affect our personal response to a given child protection case.

When training staff to work with children who have been abused, one of the first positive but painful steps that practitioners may take is to recognise that all adults have experienced power being abused over them in childhood. This may, of course, have only been in relatively minor ways. The strong feelings that this abuse of power evoked are exactly the same type of feelings that the abused child has to deal with. This realisation can, in some sense, be positive in that it leads to a sense of abused children being more like 'us' rather than 'them', and that the practitioner who has experienced abuse in childhood is not separate and different from everyone else in the child protection system.

Practice scenario 9.1

Denise was a designated teacher for her school. At the start of the course on communicating with children she voiced the concern that she could not talk with abused children because she 'hadn't had their experience of life'. At the end of the exercise which reminded participants about their childhood experience, Denise reported that she found herself a little sadder but a lot more confident about her ability to empathise and communicate with children who had experienced abuse.

Not all practitioners will have strong personal reactions to all the cases that they work with, and reactions to the same case will vary from practitioner to practitioner. One useful way of understanding this process is to compare personal reactions to abuse work to the reaction to loss. Therefore the process that practitioners may go through might closely mirror the grief process that follows a loss or bereavement (see Figure 9.1). This reaction sometimes has a consequent effect on the behaviour of the practitioner, which, in turn, has a strong effect upon multi-disciplinary cooperation in the child protection system.

Reaction	Response	Behaviour
SHOCK	'I'm totally surprised.'	Inaction.
DENIAL	'It can't have happened.'	Distancing.
ANGER	'I'm mad.'	I need to punish someone.
BARGAINING	'I can believe part of it.'	I can work on part of the problem.
GUILT	'It must be my fault.'	I shouldn't have let it happen.
SADNESS	'I'm down, I'm depressed, I'm responsible.'	I can't do anything about it.
ACCEPTANCE	'I don't like what has happened. I am not responsible for it. I can do something about it by doing my job well.'	I'm ready to work constructively with this case.
INTEGRATION	'I understand, appreciate and have come to terms with the experience I have had.'	I am including this new structure in my approach to my work.

Figure 9.1   Personal reaction to difficult child protection issues

---

Practice scenario 9.2

Mr Riaz, headteacher, had known Mr Callaghan for several years and could not believe that he might be responsible for sexually abusing Patricia, his daughter (denial). Yasmin, however, the social worker responsible for Patricia, wanted to kill him (anger) for what Patricia had told her about the details of the abuse. Yasmin and Mr Riaz struggled hard to work together over the next few weeks.

This conflict of personal reaction can also occur between practitioners in the same agency. Most notably it occurred between Drs Higgs and Irvine in Cleveland in the summer of 1987. Butler-Sloss was to comment on Dr Irvine's denial at a later date: 'Dr Irvine is not alone in finding the problem of child sexual abuse within the family deeply distressing, nor in his concern that families should not be falsely accused' (Butler-Sloss 1988, p.107).

As with a grief reaction, a practitioner may move between the stages of the process or become stuck within one stage, unable to progress. If this occurs, the practitioner would be in need of some element of outside help (see Chapter 10).

Ultimately, the most common personal reaction to a child protection case is that there is a strong personal identification on the part of one or more practitioners in the multi-disciplinary group with one or more members of the family involved (Furniss 1991). This causes the mirroring of family interactions within the inter-agency process. Family conflict is enacted in the professional sphere, with practitioners developing professional reasons for their differences, which are, in reality, based in personal reactions: 'Very quickly different professionals become identified with different aspects of the family relationships, reflecting the different life situations of individual family members ... All these different aspects of the case may seem mutually exclusive and can lead to instant conflicts-by-proxy in the professional network' (Furniss 1991, p.59). Conflict in the family is reflected in conflicting professional relationships within the system.

Inequality of power

In Chapter 3 the socio-political context within which agencies and practitioners operate was considered as a likely factor in hampering the achievement of good multi-disciplinary practice. As individuals, we still exist within the same socio-political context, even though our agency (and occasionally ourselves as well!) would prefer it if we were ageless, raceless, androgynous and neutral in every way. What actually occurs is that we bring our individual sense of self, within society, to work:

> Collaboration in all fields of work can be a breeding ground for problems associated with personal as well as professional factors. Dealing with sexual abuse, many respondents pointed out, can pose additional difficulties concerning the sensitive and volatile issues of gender, sexuality and power. (Peace 1991, p.16)

What this means is that the socio-political realities of the inequality of power in society will have a strong effect on the child protection process. Sometimes this will be reflected in predictable ways (powerful male managers oppressing women practitioners) and this can be reflected in more complex interactions.

Practice scenario 9.3

Stephen and Katrina were both experienced field social workers who were engaged in an assessment of a family where child sexual abuse was a problem. The session was devoted to the perpetrator of the abuse, as an individual. Katrina, more experienced than Stephen, was leading the session.

The perpetrator of the abuse began to describe the abusive act in detail; he developed an erection which he made no attempt to conceal. Katrina was angry and challenged the behaviour, but Stephen, as a male, had an even stronger reaction of anger, shame and utter embarrassment. He felt unable to carry on with the assessment interview. In this situation, the unpreparedness of the male worker to challenge the evidence of the abuse of male power led to the abandonment of the assessment session.

Child abuse always involves the abuse of power; the societal reaction to that abuse frequently involves the use of power by the child protection system. This manipulation of power can provoke personal reactions in practitioners, particularly in areas associated with gender, race and sexuality, where inappropriate expressions of power can evoke strong personal reactions.

Stress

The costs of stress in the helping professions has been well documented elsewhere (Thompson, Murphy and Stradling 1994). In general terms, although pressure can improve performance, when that pressure turns into stress it has an increasingly debilitating effect upon the individual or the group. The specific effects of child protection work have been identified as being particularly stressful (Fineman 1985). In child protection the particular stressors of work difficulty, high profile, the unnatural nature of the work – and even the difficult multi-disciplinary context – can be particularly stressful to the individual practitioner or group concerned.

In this context it is hypothesised that not only will severe stress affect the work that the individual practitioner undertakes with the family and child, but it will also affect the quality of input that whole teams can put into the multi-disciplinary effort.

Practice scenario 9.4

East Central District team was going through a stressful period: there was a shortage of managers, of staff members, and an overload of work. Added to this, several key members of the team were going through periods of severe personal pressure at home. The team became very inward-looking, all requests for assistance from the multi-disciplinary system were seen as a burden, and the relationship between the team and their partners in the child protection system deteriorated markedly.

During the next year, new managers and staff arrived and the personal pressures that the staff were suffering lessened considerably. This reduction of stress allowed the team to gradually look outwards; subsequently the relationships with other teams in the child protection system improved considerably.

Some in the system gave the credit for this improvement to the new members of staff who had arrived. In reality, however, the improvement in multi-disciplinary performance owed much more to the beneficial effects of stress reduction on the whole team.

Conclusion

If we seek to improve multi-disciplinary child protection work, we should pay attention not only to the effects of the structural blocks to that work, but also to the effects of the personal blocks to good practice.

Of these, the most powerful are those of personal history, stress, and the personal effects of inequalities of power.

Child abuse work touches the personal as well as the professional parts of the individual and the team. As Chapter 10 will show, it is essential to resource and look after those personal parts so that multi-disciplinary cooperation can develop to its full potential.

10 Towards good practice

The previous nine chapters have outlined the complexity of the child protection process, the natural blocks to multi-disciplinary communication and cooperation, and the differing roles and perspectives of the main practitioner groups who are involved. This chapter is about carrying out multi-disciplinary work well, by achieving a high level of mutual understanding, cooperation and action. Good multi-disciplinary work is important in that it is one of the essential components of good child protection practice.

It is the contention of this book that another component – child protection procedures – has been exaggerated within the British system to a high degree. Procedures establish the parameters of multi-disciplinary interaction, they do not regulate the quality or substance of that multi-disciplinary effort.

The child protection task is inherently difficult. Good multi-disciplinary work cannot make that difficult task easy; rather, it makes it easier for the staff who practise in this way to accomplish the task and, most important, it increases the likelihood that the task will be accomplished to a high standard.

Good practice

If a practitioner or an agency is a member of the child protection system, they have no choice but to work in a multi-disciplinary fashion: their membership of the system entails some amount of inter-agency activity. The true test of good practice is how well and how fully the issues and demands of inter-agency practice are taken on board. Through the process of communication, planning, action and evaluation there is a continuum of multi-disciplinary effort that the practitioner or agency group will find themselves involved in.

Peace (1991) compares multi-disciplinary work to a long filament of plaited string – where the work is progressing badly, the strands of the string will be loosely connected in a haphazard fashion, and the filament will be weak. Where the work is progressing well, the strands will be closely interwoven and well-coordinated, and the filament itself will be strong.

Poor multi-disciplinary effort involves either:

- ignoring the multi-disciplinary context of child protection completely – in Furniss's terms (1991), failing to acknowledge that all child protection tasks and roles are cumulative and affect one another, or
- attempting to reframe all perspectives in terms of one dominant way of thinking – the 'colonisation' of the multi-disciplinary effort by one powerful perspective or agency view (see Chapter 1).

At its simplest, good multi-disciplinary communication and understanding involves the appreciation of other perspectives and priorities, which, in its turn, presumes the ability to stand in the shoes of other practitioners and see child abuse from their point of view. If a prime element of child-centred practice is to be able to see the work from the child's point of view, the ability to appreciate the process from the point of view of the other practitioner is one path to more effective multi-disciplinary practice.

The practitioner

It is at the level of the practitioner that child protection work directly affects the consumers of the service – children and their parents. Even if multi-disciplinary relationships are positive at all other levels, if they are poor at this stage the effect on the consumers of the service is severe. It is the responsibility of the individual practitioner to develop those parts of her practice that she knows will stimulate the cooperation essential to good practice. Therefore she must develop understanding of the roles and perspectives of other practitioners involved, and be able to explain the reality of her own perspective to her colleagues from other agencies. She should develop the ability to work in an inclusive, open way using those personal skills that include and give value to the input of other practitioners. The practitioner should be clear about her opinion, assertive in putting it forward, but also interested in reaching compromise with the views of others. She should seek to develop her theoretical understanding of the subject area, but not attempt to become the established 'expert' – that exclusive state that can so often move the practitioner away from the appreciation of the contribution of others.

The reward to the practitioner for the development of these skills is not just in the improved service which would be offered to the client, but in the significant reduction of some of the major stressors in her child protection work. This involves, in particular, reducing the sense of isolation, sole responsibility and lack of support which often make the child protection task significantly stressful to the individual practitioner.

Human issues

Some of the most important factors in achieving good multi-disciplinary work do not involve highly technical, complicated issues of inter-agency coordination, but rather are to do with the human issues that staff bring to the child protection process. When practitioners are asked about the factors that they value about good multi-disciplinary cooperation, it is these human factors that they mention most frequently.

Inclusion/welcoming

The most obvious factor in facilitating good multi-disciplinary communication is that the appropriate practitioners from relevant agencies feel included in the multi-disciplinary interaction and that they, and their information, are welcomed into the multi-disciplinary process.

Practice scenario 10.1

Marie was a teacher in a junior school. During a training course she explained to the group why she felt so positively about the core group of workers that she was involved in: 'It all began badly. I was not invited to the first core group meeting and felt very left out. After that, I got a phone call from both the health visitor and the social worker, who apologised for having left me out, and re-scheduled the next meeting to a time that was convenient for me. At that next meeting they were both very welcoming, they filled me in on what had happened at the last meeting, and made me feel like part of the team.'

This welcoming and inclusion of Marie into the core group cost her colleagues very little in terms of time and energy, but left her as an enthusiastic, committed member of the multi-disciplinary team.

Communication/listening

As practitioners in helping professions, we value inter-personal skills when working with our clients. Unfortunately, we do not always extend these inter-personal skills to situations where we find ourselves working with colleagues from other agencies.

The two most simple skills that can improve multi-disciplinary cooperation are communication and listening. Listening involves us giving our full attention to our colleagues, finding out both what they want to say and what they mean (rather than what we think they want to say and what we think they mean!). Communication is about the willingness and ability to be able to communicate our meaning in an intelligible fashion back to them.

Practice scenario 10.2

Naseema was a health visitor who was trying to explain her very positive relationship with a local paediatrician, Dr Bateson: 'I think that it started with the sense that she was listening to me. She looked at me, she concentrated on what I was saying and she asked me a question at the end that showed that she understood what I was going on about. I knew that she wasn't thinking about her next meeting, or what she was going to make for her tea!'

Valuing

Valuing is being able to give importance to the opinion, work and overall contribution of the different practitioners who are involved in the particular piece of work. Confidence can be very badly shaken by the feeling that our multi-disciplinary colleagues do not appreciate the work that we are attempting to do, or consider it to be insignificant. This valuing of others' contribution can be very inexpensive in terms of time and energy, but very cost-effective in terms of group morale.

Practice scenario 10.3

Janet was a woman police officer who enjoyed a particularly good relationship with a team of social workers. She explained that, after her first piece of work with the team, the senior social worker had rung her up and said that he would value her advice about another case that was proving problematic: 'I felt ten feet tall, really worthwhile and very pleased. After that, nothing was too much trouble when I was working with his team.'

Respect

Respect is another basic human value that is seen as very positive in multi-disciplinary work. It seems to be a combination of two factors: the first involves respect for an individual's personal and professional identity, the second is closely allied to the first – it is avoiding demeaning or 'putting down' the differences or queries that the individual practitioner brings.

Stress care/practical help

The last human issue that it is important to consider when trying to improve multi-disciplinary cooperation is staff stress. That child protection work is stressful there seems little doubt (Butler-Sloss 1988; Furniss 1991; Thompson, Murphy and Stradling 1994). But, although we are willing to consider the effects of stress on the individual practitioner, we are less good at evaluating its effects on the multi-disciplinary group. The possibility is that, with any serious child protection matter, one or more members of the multi-disciplinary team might be experiencing considerable work-related stress. This, in turn, might affect their participation in the process (see Chapter 9).

What can we do about this? It is not appropriate for us to attempt to 'counsel' them ourselves (but it is helpful to encourage them to use the counselling services that are available within the system). It *is* appropriate, however, for us to take the following simple steps to assist them in dealing with that pressure:

- Recognise the potentially stressful nature of the case without attempting to underplay or minimise the stress that it might cause.
- Allow time for our colleagues to talk about how they are feeling.
- Do small, practical things that might reduce the stressful nature of the case, or might just make our colleagues feel valued and

looked after – for example, if the threat of violence was the major stressor, offering to do a joint visit, notifying the Police that they might be needed, or just phoning after the event, might prove helpful to the other members of the group.

Practice scenario 10.4

The core group were finding the Curran family very difficult to cope with. The family were resistant to outside intervention and, on occasion, could be abusive to the practitioners involved. Quite early in the work, the group had shared their home as well as work numbers. They found themselves phoning each other at the end of difficult visits, not just to share information, but also to 'let off steam' with someone who knew just how difficult the work could be. They found that this helped to boost their confidence and their coping skills in the middle of a very stressful piece of work.

These human factors or skills are an accepted part of our helping the consumers of our service. By extending them to members of the multi-disciplinary group we automatically improve the group's potential for positive work.

Overcoming the structural blocks to professional cooperation

Chapter 3 outlined the substantial structural blocks to effective multi-disciplinary working. These were outlined, not to suggest that good multi-disciplinary work was impossible, but rather to suggest that it is by recognising and overcoming these blocks (rather than by ignoring them) that we can improve our practice.

The series of structural blocks or obstacles that impede multi-disciplinary work include the differences that are involved in:

- perspective
- role
- stereotyping
- priority
- training
- structure and power
- language
- traditional ways of working.

These differences, these blocks to communication and action, are not totally removable – they exist as an inevitable by-product of the boundaries between different agencies and practitioner groups; their presence is therefore inevitable. However, the power of these blocks to affect practice is very variable and, if recognised and overcome by the practitioner as well as the agency, their power is significantly reduced.

Rather than deal with each block individually, there are a number of steps that we can take collectively to reduce their power.

Gaining multi-disciplinary knowledge

We all harbour a basic ignorance of how other practitioner groups work, think and speak. However, save for joining those different groups, it would be impossible to learn all there is to know about them ('shadowing', where a practitioner joins a different practitioner group for a short period of time in order to learn more about them, can be used to facilitate greater understanding). It is important, therefore, recognising our basic ignorance, that we try to accumulate the minimum amount of relevant knowledge. This would enable us to understand the behaviour and communication of the other practitioner well enough to be able to understand what they say and conceptualise what they might do, with regard to a particular case.

For example, with regard to language, it would be impossible to appreciate *all* the technical language that most practitioner groups employ, but it is important to understand the words and concepts which describe their involvement in child protection work, and particularly those words that are used to express the seriousness of the abuse under discussion. In a conversation between a police officer and a teacher, it is not essential for each to understand the detail of all the other agency's language and procedure, but it is important for each to have a basic appreciation of the other's child protection language (what is a 'designated teacher' or a 'Schedule 1 offender'?), procedure (what happens next in court?) and hierarchy (who do I talk to about your work?).

Willingness to ask the 'naïve' question

If the combatting of ignorance about other agencies is the way to reduce blocks to multi-disciplinary working, one of the most useful techniques the practitioner can utilise is the insistence on asking the naïve question. This technique makes a virtue out of asking for an explanation when you don't understand, you half-understand, or when you do understand but know that others do not:

'I hate to appear ignorant, but would you mind explaining to me . . . '

'I'm sorry to interrupt your flow, could you help me to understand . . . '

'I feel awfully naïve, but could you just explain that word to me, I don't think that I have its meaning quite clear in my head . . . '

Once this technique has been practised it is invaluable in inter-agency discussions, and it usually brings with it the utter gratitude and approval of other practitioners who also do not understand but were too shy to ask!

Understanding and valuing the other perspective

Once the knowledge about the other practitioner's role and perspective has been gained, good multi-disciplinary work demands that this be put into practice. This means that the differences that individual practitioners bring must be included in the multi-disciplinary process rather than ignored, bulldozed or pushed into a corner. Some strong element of compromise is suggested here rather than seeking a 'right' or 'superior' answer.

The dissemination of knowledge

The practitioner needs to be able to communicate, in an intelligible fashion, the essential characteristics of her own agency, role and language to the other practitioners in the system. This closely reflects the ability to communicate. It implies the ability to share the information that you possess in such a way that colleagues appreciate what you are saying, what it means in terms of your agency, and its pertinence with regard to the particular case.

The ability to practise in an inclusive, multi-disciplinary fashion

This is the key to overcoming structural blocks to multi-disciplinary work. Although poor practice can seldom be laid at the door of the individual practitioner, positive multi-disciplinary practice can be stimulated by individuals taking control over the multi-disciplinary element of their own practice. The ability to practise in a multi-disciplinary, inclusive way involves a change of thinking. This change moves from the position of 'how can my agency sort out this child protection problem?' to 'how can we help the multi-disciplinary team begin to address this problem?'. It involves beginning to think about the work in a multi-agency fashion, to develop a cognitive map that is truly multi-disciplinary in its focus (not 'first my agency – then the rest').

Dealing with conflict

When the structural blocks to communication have been overcome and the human issues around working together have been dealt with, the potential for conflict between practitioners or agencies is still present. But it is likely that this conflict is concerned with professional differences of opinion or judgment, or a reflection of differences of interest within the family. It is important, according to Furniss (1991), that these differences are not minimised or ignored, but recognised, confronted and addressed, so that the issues in question can be resolved. If this is to happen it is essential that the practitioner or agency concerned:

- Behave in an assertive way by explaining the reasons behind a judgment or opinion to the rest of the multi-disciplinary group.
- Never attempt to take over another agency's role or sphere of activity.
- Use the technique of predicting positive or negative outcomes for the proposed courses of action.
- Where possible, aim for compromise if not consensus. Where there is a sense that one side has 'won' or 'bulldozed' a decision through, the probability of positive multi-disciplinary cooperation being achieved around that decision is extremely low.

Practice scenario 10.5

Joseph was an experienced case conference chairperson. During the decision-making stage of a conference on the H family, which he was chairing, he sensed that all was not well. One very articulate practitioner was describing his preferred outcome; everyone else was strangely silent. The chairperson sensed disagreement, stopped the conference and asked the participants to explore these differences. The conference went on for another half-hour but, at the end, a compromise solution was reached that had the full backing of the multi-disciplinary group.

Further levels of responsibility within the system

Within any child protection system, the level and effectiveness of multi-disciplinary cooperation will not be static but will alter, improve or deteriorate over time. Different geographical areas can enjoy different levels of multi-disciplinary relationships, and it is possible to have effective collaboration at the level of the practitioner and at the same time have poor multi-disciplinary relationships at more senior levels. Butler-Sloss (1988) discovered that, in Cleveland in 1987, the relationships at ACPC and practitioner level were relatively positive; it was at the middle management and senior practitioner level that cooperation had broken down.

Practice scenario 10.6

Bigport Social Services Department was split into two – North and South Districts. Relationships at the middle management level between agencies in North District were distinctly frosty, with little inter-agency communication, apart from strongly argued disputes about resources and control. In South District, on the other hand, relationships were excellent, with frequent communication between managers from different agencies, and disputes that were resolved in a low-key, amicable manner. Maureen, a junior manager from South District, was promoted to the senior manager's position in North District. Within two months the frosty relationships had begun to thaw; Maureen had made personal contact with management staff in the other agencies, and had organised a lunch that was aimed at improving multi-disciplinary relationships.

The search for good multi-disciplinary child protection practice has differing implications for different groups of staff as well as practitioners. These implications frequently depend on their position within the system. It is important to recognise that responsibility for good multi-disciplinary practice does not only belong to the individual practitioner, but extends to other members of the system, and, in the end, to whole systems and those who control those systems.

The chairperson

The child protection process is punctuated by multi-disciplinary meetings. These include the planning meeting, the initial and review conference and the core group meeting. These meetings are usually coordinated and facilitated by full-time chairpersons or by staff taking the chair on an *ad hoc* basis. In either case, their role in facilitating good multi-disciplinary communication, planning and action is essential to good multi-disciplinary practice. The research by Bingley Miller, Fisher and Sinclair (1993) has confirmed the crucial influence of chairpersons in guiding the judgments made at multi-disciplinary meetings.

The chairperson should:

- create a positive atmosphere for multi-disciplinary communication
- facilitate the sharing of information, discussion and planning around a particular case
- encourage 'safe' disagreement and help participants to reach a satisfactory compromise (see Practice scenario 10.5)
- encourage sharing and seek to prevent the domination of the meeting by one practitioner or single agency
- ensure that the meeting keeps within the policy and guidance established within the area, and
- not attempt to guide or pressure the meeting into a particular plan of action.

Most frequently the chairperson is employed by the Social Services Department. It is important for the chairperson to establish and demonstrate some degree of independence from that department.

The position of chairperson is one that is very demanding and exposed, yet it is common for that group of staff not to receive the resources (in terms of staff care and supervision) that they require. Good multi-disciplinary practice includes the proper resourcing of all child protection staff, especially those members of staff who facilitate the whole process.

The single-disciplinary trainer

The responsibility of the (single-disciplinary) child protection trainer towards good practice is not just to give high-quality child protection training, but also to keep the multi-disciplinary nature of child protection at the forefront of the training agenda. This could be accomplished by:

- attempting to deliver training to multi-disciplinary groups
- forming cooperative alliances with trainers in other agencies
- using trainers from different agency backgrounds

- including within the training information and experiential elements about the multi-disciplinary context of the system, and
- being aware, not just of single-disciplinary training needs, but also of the wider needs of the whole multi-disciplinary system.

Above all, the trainer must work and train in an inclusive, multi-disciplinary fashion, rather than in a narrow, single-disciplinary context. Although it will always be necessary for some training to take place in single-disciplinary groups, it is essential that all practitioners learn not just about the particular subject area, but also about the implications for the multi-disciplinary child protection process.

The multi-disciplinary trainer

It is becoming increasingly fashionable in the British system for multi-disciplinary trainers to be employed, often directly financed and controlled by the ACPC. This type of trainer has several advantages when it comes to the promotion of multi-disciplinary practice:

- The trainer operates in the multi-disciplinary system with a multi-disciplinary focus.
- The trainer usually has a close relationship with the ACPC, either through the main committee or through the training sub-committee.
- The trainer may also take on the role of giving feedback to the ACPC about the issues and difficulties that are arising at ground level, and about how well its staff are currently fulfilling their child protection duties.

The manager

Managers within the child protection system supervise the work of the individual practitioner and create and shape, via the ACPC, multi-disciplinary child protection policy. This is the level at which the policy, tone and culture of working practice is established. The manager holds the responsibility for trying to ensure that good multi-disciplinary practice is encouraged at all levels of their agency.

All of the proposals for good practice that are discussed for the practitioner are either directly relevant to the manager (for example, communication, listening and the dissemination of knowledge) or else can be proposed by the manager as being essential to the practice of the team (for example, valuing and respecting other agencies' perspectives).

To do this it is important that the manager accepts that child protection work is a shared process, that positive working attitudes towards other agencies should be encouraged, and that unilateral ways of behaving be frowned upon. Managers can model those positive attitudes to the staff in their own agency in their work with their colleagues from other agencies. In particular, they have the responsibility for the positive resolution of inter-agency disputes. Most important of all, the manager should not try to establish unilateral management control over the child protection process (the 'colonial' position), but should be prepared to share management control with the wider agency system.

The ACPC

One of the strongest elements of the development of positive multidisciplinary practice would be for the ACPC to take unto itself a more dynamic, coordinating role in the wider child protection process. This new role would act to reduce the individualistic tendencies of its member agencies:

> Many wish to see ACPCs taking on the role of regulators who ensure that all agencies work together to achieve the best outcomes for children ... ACPCs could play a similar role where families and children express dissatisfaction with the process or outcomes of case conferences. At a strategic level it would also mean ACPCs taking a lead in handling some of the inequalities caused by class, gender and race discrimination. (Evans and Miller 1993, p.19)

Evans and Miller's vision of the ACPC of the future is one in which the committee becomes active, not just in promoting agency coordination, but also in becoming the investigator and arbiter in cases where the system has failed to work, and becoming the commissioner of all child protection provision.

But such a development is at least partly dependent on the ACPC achieving some financial viability, freedom from dependence on particular agencies, and a clear mandate to develop a powerful coordinating role: 'ACPCs cannot continue to operate on the basis of goodwill alone. Explicit funding arrangements and clear terms of reference for ACPCs are essential' (Evans and Miller 1993, p.20).

There are some steps that ACPCs could take that would begin to develop a position beyond its constituent parts:

- Ensuring that the committee itself modelled cooperative multi-disciplinary work, with clear communication, ways of resolving conflict and true sharing of power between the constituent agencies.
- Developing multi-disciplinary services for the whole system that are directly accountable to the ACPC. This might include a training service, a staff care service, a library and resource base and a research and development service.
- Developing ways of directly communicating with the multi-disciplinary workforce. This might include a direct communication channel from workforce to ACPC – an ACPC newsletter or annual ACPC information days.

Although the ACPC will always be dependent on its constituent parts, its future successful development depends on its ability to develop its own independent identity and existence as a body that is more than the sum of its member organisations.

The political system/resourcing child protection work

It would be a mistake to presume that good practice of a consistent and sustained variety can be achieved by practitioners or ACPCs acting on their own. Within each area it is the responsibility of the wider agency and political system to begin to provide the resources, the political will and the positive model of inter-agency cooperation to promote good practice. This can be achieved in a number of ways:

- beginning to think and act in a multi- rather than single-disciplinary way
- giving the ACPC and other coordinating bodies the power and the finance that they need to promote multi-disciplinary work, and
- beginning to resource the multi-disciplinary child protection effort via multi-disciplinary training programmes, multi-disciplinary staff care schemes and multi-disciplinary libraries and resource facilities.

But this positive promotion of the context of good practice cannot be achieved just at the local level. As well as local systems having responsibility for its promotion, it is essential that the political system, or the controllers of that political system, recognise the importance of positive multi-disciplinary practice.

At a local level, it is frequently the elected members that have the final control over child protection resources and, to some extent, the crucial developments in local practice. It is important that these members understand the requirements and advantages of good multi-disciplinary cooperation, resisting the temptation to engage in inter-agency competitiveness.

At a national level, it is most important that politicians and senior civil servants do more than offer helpful advice in government circulars. It would be of considerable assistance to the multi-disciplinary system if they were able:

- to instruct local agencies to defer some powers to local ACPCs
- to fund, or instruct local agencies to fund, multi-disciplinary coordinating bodies, particularly the ACPC, and
- to model good multi-disciplinary work by establishing good inter-agency cooperation concerning child protection work between different government departments.

Equalising primary interventions

The final step in improving multi-disciplinary cooperation might involve challenging those factors that lead to imbalance within the system. The British system suffers from a chronic imbalance between the protective and legal interventions on the one hand and the preventative and therapeutic interventions on the other. This can also lead to dysfunctional differences in power between the different practitioner groups involved in the process. Good practice should lead to the recognition that all interventions – preventative, protective, legal and therapeutic – are all essential to good practice.

Good practice may mean a move to equalise interventions by emphasising the 'neglected' interventions (preventative and therapeutic) at the expense of those that are already powerful (protective and legal). This will lead to a change in the relative power of those groups who currently work in those less powerful interventions.

Conclusion

In the British child protection system, multi-disciplinary work is compulsory. Unfortunately, doing multi-disciplinary work well, and striving for good multi-disciplinary practice, is not.

Poor practice is shown by grudging communication with, and lack of inclusion of, other agencies. It is also shown by the conviction that 'my agency or practitioner group knows best, and we have nothing to gain from the input of other agencies or practitioners'.

The journey towards good practice begins with the acknowledgement that all agencies and practitioner groups have something to offer to child protection work, and is followed by striving to let others participate in the fullest possible way in the process, combatting the natural urge to think and work in unilateral ways.

The responsibility for achieving good practice is a shared one. It does not rest with one agency or one particular practitioner group. Neither does it rest solely with individual practitioners or their managers – although the latter have an important role to play, they share that crucial responsibility with ACPCs, local childcare systems and with local and national political systems.

The level of achievement of good practice will vary over time, place and even between cases. It is important that we constantly strive to improve practice at all levels, remembering that positive multi-disciplinary interaction is re-created with each new interaction and each new case that comes into the system.

Positive multi-disciplinary practice is not easy to achieve. In some ways the unilateral, single-agency path is more easy to encompass, to organise and to control. However, good child protection work itself is not easy to accomplish, but becomes more attainable in the context of positive multi-disciplinary practice.

11 Conclusion

This book began with the examination of the British government's belief that multi-disciplinary cooperation and action was one of the essential parts of good child protection practice. I have not attempted to question that belief; in fact I have strengthened it by asserting that, in spite of considerable international differences, the need for effective multi-disciplinary cooperation remains constant.

Where I have argued with government wisdom is in its assumption that good multi-disciplinary child protection practice is simple to achieve, and that poor multi-disciplinary practice is often the fault of the individual practitioner. In fact, I have claimed that good multi-disciplinary practice is *difficult* to achieve, not least because the powerful, structural blocks to that inter-disciplinary cooperation are unrecognised and ignored.

I have attempted a thorough examination of these blocks and suggested practical and professional ways of minimising their power. I have challenged the belief that poor multi-disciplinary practice is always the responsibility of the individual practitioner or agency, and have laid the responsibility for poor multi-disciplinary work squarely at the door of the system itself (even though, conversely, much positive practice can be stimulated by the individual practitioner or manager).

The child protection task is complex and difficult. Chapter 1 examined the difficulties of achieving a common definition and understanding of child abuse, and proposed a series of action perspectives and primary interventions to help explain the different ways of understanding and of seeing abuse. It claimed that the complicated nature of child protection work is allied to a habit of ignorance of the role and perspectives of other practitioners within the system. To help to combat this factor, Chapter 2 examined, in some detail, the complex working of the child protection system in England and Wales, and went on to highlight the particularly difficult points of inter-professional interaction. Chapter 3 went further by outlining the significant structural blocks that must be overcome before inter-agency collaboration can be established, suggesting that these blocks are often minimised or ignored rather than confronted and dealt with.

Chapters 4–8 took a further step to dispel inter-agency ignorance by giving consideration to the particular inputs of the different agencies and groups of child protection practitioners who participate in the process, and made clear that each practitioner group holds a particular and separate role and perspective with regard to child protection. They also outlined, within agencies, the substantial differences that can occur between different practitioner groups, and went on to discuss how child protection work has managed to 'fit' with the basic ethos and organisation of the agencies and practitioner groups within the system. No agency or practitioner group brings to the child protection process a blank page – each holds its own perspective, based on its primary intervention, its historical role in society and the ethos of its own practitioner group. These chapters have also encouraged the *understanding* of these differences in order that the pressures that affect different agencies and practitioner groups can be fully understood. The relative positions of the agencies involved in child protection work were also considered, and the effect of the increasing power of the legal system on child protection matters was critically examined.

After this substantial discussion around structure, agency and practitioner issues, Chapter 9 reminded us of the personal dimension in child protection work. The effects that child abuse work can have on the practitioner, as a person, have been examined with a view to exploring how these personal effects change and shape how the practitioner engages in the multi-disciplinary system.

Chapter 10 drew together the key issues from the previous chapters and used them to describe how good multi-disciplinary practice may be achieved and how the different parts of the system might make their contribution to the achievement of that good practice.

I have claimed that there is no alternative to doing child protection work in a multi-disciplinary way. No one agency is able to combine the necessary multiplicity of tasks and functions within itself, and it seems unlikely that a new child protection agency will be created to undertake all child protection work. Child protection work is difficult enough in its own right but, when combined with the intrinsic complexities of multi-disciplinary cooperation, it is a task that is hedged round with difficulty. But, as this work has shown, these difficulties are *not* insurmountable. They can be overcome at many different levels of practice – the practitioner, the manager, the trainer, the case conference chairperson, the politician and the ACPC all have their part to play.

Perhaps this has been the most important message that has been contained within this book: it is not the responsibility of any one group of staff to promote good multi-disciplinary working, but it is the responsibility of all, from government minister to basic-grade practitioner or volunteer, to ensure that the children and families involved in child protection matters enjoy the benefits that true multi-disciplinary cooperation and action can achieve.

I have not sought to deny the importance of multi-disciplinary procedures or the efficacy of developing individual child protection skills – both are of crucial significance to the process. However, as claimed in the Introduction, we are in danger of increasing our knowledge about the rules and skills of the 'game' whilst still retaining a large degree of ignorance about the team in which we are involved.

I have consistently maintained that child protection work is a multi-disciplinary (not a single-disciplinary) process. The essential prerequisites to true competency and effectiveness in this process are to develop a knowledge and understanding of those who are working on the same multi-disciplinary team and to develop the trust and respect necessary to share that work beyond the narrow boundaries of our individual agency and practitioner group.

References

Abrahams, N., Casey, K. and Daro, D. (1992), 'Teachers' knowledge, attitudes and beliefs about child abuse and its prevention', *Child Abuse and Neglect*, **16**(2), 229–38.

ADSS (1989), *Workforce Survey*, Association of Directors of Social Services.

Allan, M., Bhavnani, R. and French, K. (1992), *Promoting Women*, London: Social Services Inspectorate/HMSO.

Archard, A. (1993), *Children: Rights and Childhood*, London: Routledge.

Aries, P. (1962), *Centuries of Childhood*, London: Jonathan Cape.

Barford, R. (1993), *Children's View of Child Protection Social Work*, Social Work Monographs, Norwich: University of East Anglia.

Behlmer, G. (1982), *Child Abuse and Moral Reform in England 1870–1908*, Stanford, Calif: Stanford University Press.

Bingley Miller, L., Fisher, T. and Sinclair, I. (1993), 'Decisions to register children as at risk of abuse', *Social Work and Social Science Review*, **4**(2), 101–18.

Blom-Cooper, L. (1985), *A Child in Trust: The report of the panel of inquiry into the circumstances surrounding the death of Jasmine Beckford*, London: Borough of Brent.

Blom-Cooper, L. (1987), *A Child in Mind: Protection of children in a responsible society. The report of the commission of inquiry into the circumstances surrounding the death of Kimberley Carlile*, London: Borough of Greenwich.

Butler-Sloss, E. (1988), *Report of the Inquiry into Child Abuse in Cleveland, 1987*, London: HMSO.

CAAC (1992), *Children Act Advisory Committee Annual Report 1991/2*, London: HMSO.

CAAC (1993), *Children Act Advisory Committee Annual Report 1992/3*, London: HMSO.

Campbell, B. (1988), *Unofficial Secrets*, London: Virago.

Christopherson, J. (1989), 'European child-abuse management systems', in Stevenson, O. (ed.), *Child Abuse: Professional Practice and Public Policy*, London: Harvester Wheatsheaf.

Cohen, P. (1993), 'In the frame', *Community Care*, October 1993.

Corby, B. (1987), *Working With Child Abuse*, Milton Keynes: Open University Press.

Dale, P., Davies, M., Morrison, T. and Waters, J. (1986), *Dangerous Families*, London: Routledge.

DES (1988), *Child Protection in Schools*, London: Department of Education and Science, Circular 4/88.

DHSS (1974), *Report of the committee of inquiry into the care and supervision provided in relation to Maria Colwell*, London: HMSO.

DHSS (1983), *Child Abuse – A Study of Inquiry Reports 1973–1981*, London: HMSO.

DHSS (1986), *Child Abuse – Working Together: A draft guide to arrangements for interagency cooperation for the protection of children*, London: HMSO.

DHSS (1988), *Working Together*, London: HMSO.

Dingwall, R., Eekelaar, J. and Murray, T. (1983), *The Protection of Children, State Intervention and Family Life*, Oxford: Basil Blackwell.

DoH (1991a), *Child Abuse: A Study of Inquiry Reports 1980–1989*, London: HMSO.

DoH (1991b), *Family Placements, The Children Act 1989, Guidance and Regulations*, **3**, London: HMSO.

DoH (1991c), *Working Together Under the 1989 Children Act*, London: HMSO.

Evans, M. and Miller, C. (1993), *Partnership in Child Protection*, London: Office for Public Management/National Institute of Social Work.

Fineman, S. (1985), *Social Work Stress and Intervention*, Aldershot: Gower.

Fox Harding, L. (1991), *Perspectives in Child Care Policy*, London: Longman.

Freeman, M. (1984), *State, Law and the Family*, London: Tavistock.

FRG (1986), *FRG's response to the DHSS consultation paper: Child Abuse – Working Together*, London: Family Rights Group.

Furniss, T. (1991), *The Multi-professional Handbook of Child Sexual Abuse*, London: Routledge.

Gadsby Waters, J. (1992), *The Supervision of Child Protection Work*, Aldershot: Avebury.

Giller, H., Gormley, C. and Williams, P. (1992), *The Effectiveness of Child Protection Procedures*, Nantwich: Social Information Systems.

GMC (1993), *Confidentiality and Child Abuse*, London: General Medical Council, July, No. 3.

Gordon, L. (1989), *Heroes of Their Own Lives*, London: Virago.

Gouldner, A. (1954), *Patterns of Industrial Bureaucracy*, New York, NY: Free Press.

Hallett, C. and Birchall, E. (1992), *Coordination and Child Protection – A Review of the Literature*, London: HMSO.

Hearn, J. (1990), ' "Child abuse" and men's violence', in The Violence Against Children Study Group, *Taking Child Abuse Seriously*, London: Unwin Hyman.

Hinchcliffe, D. (1993), *Child Protection Under Threat*, London: Labour Party Publications.

Home Office (1988), *The Investigation of Child Sexual Abuse*, London: Home Office, Circular 52/1988.

Home Office/DoH (1992), *The Memorandum of Good Practice*, London: HMSO.

House of Lords (1986), *Gillick v. West Norfolk and Wisbech Area Health Authority*, 1 AC 112.

Howe, D. (1986), *Social Workers and Their Practice in Welfare Bureaucracies*, Aldershot: Gower.

Howe, E. (1992), *The Quality of Care: A Report of the Residential Staff's Inquiry*, London: LGMB.

Kempe, C. H., Silverman, F. N., Steele, B. F., Droegmueller, W. and Silver, H.

K. (1962), 'The Battered Child Syndrome', *Journal of the American Medical Association*, **181**, 17–22.

Kotch, J. B., Chalmers, D. J., Fanslow, J. L., Marshall, S. and Langley, J. D. (1993), 'Morbidity and Death Due to Child Abuse in New Zealand', *Child Abuse and Neglect*, **17**(2), 233–47.

Leicestershire County Council (1993), *Management responses to complaints and evidence of abuse, malpractice and other related matters in Leicestershire in the light of the trial of Frank Beck and other Child Care Officers for the period 1973–1976*, Leicester: Leicestershire County Council.

Levy, A. and Kahan, B. (1991), *The Pindown Experience and the Protection of Children: The Report of the Staffordshire Child Care Inquiry 1990*, Stafford: Staffordshire County Council.

LLSARC (1989), *The Doreen Aston Report*, London: Borough of Lewisham.

Lyon, C. and de Cruz, R. (1993), *Child Abuse* (2nd edn), Bristol: Jordan.

Metropolitan Police/London Borough of Bexley (1987), *The Bexley Experiment – Final Report*, London: HMSO.

Moore, J. (1992), *The ABC of Child Protection*, Aldershot: Ashgate.

Murphy, M. (1991), 'Pressure Points', *Social Work Today*, 13 June.

Murphy, M. (1995), 'Child Protection Specialist Units', Liverpool University: PhD thesis (forthcoming).

NCH (1979), *Who Cares?*, London: National Children's Homes.

Norman, A. and Brown, C. (1992), Foreword, in Cloke, C. and Naish, J. (eds), *Key Issues in Child Protection for Health Visitors and Nurses*, London: NSPCC/ Longman.

The Office of Population, Censuses and Surveys (OPCS) (1992), *The British Census 1991*, London: HMSO.

O'Hagan, K. (1989), *Working With Child Sexual Abuse*, Milton Keynes: Open University Press.

Papatheophilou, A. (1990), 'Child protection in Greece', in Sale, A. and Davies, M. (eds), *Child Protection Policies and Practice in Europe*, London: NSPCC.

Parkinson, J. (1992), 'Supervision vs control', in Cloke, C. and Naish, J. (eds), *Key Issues in Child Protection for Health Visitors and Nurses*, London: NSPCC/ Longman.

Parton, N. (1985), *The Politics of Child Abuse*, Basingstoke: Macmillan.

Parton, N. (1991), *Governing the Family*, Basingstoke: Macmillan.

Peace, G. (1991), *Inter-professional Collaboration, Professional and Personal Perspectives, Part 2*, Manchester: Boys' and Girls' Welfare Society.

Pickett, J. (individual interview, 2 April 1990) in Murphy, M. (1995), 'Child Protection Specialist Units', Liverpool University: PhD thesis (forthcoming).

Pickett, J. and Maton, A. (1979), 'The multi-disciplinary team in an urban setting: the special unit concept', *Child Abuse and Neglect*, **3**, 115–21.

Plotnikoff, J. (1993), *The Child Witness Pack: Helping Children to Cope*, London: NSPCC/Childline.

RCP (1991), *Physical Signs of Sexual Abuse in Children*, London: Royal College of Physicians.

Richards, M., Payne, C. and Shepperd, A. (1990), *Staff Supervision in Child Protection Work*, London: National Institute of Social Work.

Rooney, B. (1980), 'Active Mistakes – A Grass Roots Report', *Multi-Racial Social Work*, No. 1, 43–54.

Rouf, K. (1990), 'My self in echoes. My voice in song', in Bannister, A., Barrett, K. and Shearer, E. (eds), *Listening to Children*, London: NSPCC/Longman.

Sale, A. and Davies, M. (eds) (1990), *Child Protection Policies and Practice in Europe*, London: NSPCC.

Sariola, H. and Uutela, A. (1993), 'The prevalence and context of family violence against children in Finland', *Child Abuse and Neglect*, **16**(6), 823–32.

Scrine, J. (1991), 'Child abuse – Do social work students get enough practice experience?', *Practice*, **5**(2), 153–9.

Shepherd, S. (1991), 'Aspects of the Children Act – A Medical Perspective', *Health Trends*, **23**(2), 51–3.

Skaff, L. (1988), 'Child maltreatment coordinating committees for effective service delivery', *Child Welfare*, **LXVII**(3), 217–30.

Speight, N. (1993), 'Non-accidental injury', in Meadow, R. (ed.), *The ABC of Child Abuse*, London: British Medical Journal.

Spencer, J. and Flin, R. (1990), *The Evidence of Children*, London: Blackstone.

Stone, M. (1990), *Child Protection Work – A Professional Guide*, London: Ventura.

Thatcher, M. (1990), *NCH George Thomas Lecture*, London: National Children's Homes.

Thomas, T. (1994), *The Police and Social Workers*, Aldershot: Gower.

Thompson, N., Murphy, M. and Stradling, S. (1994), *Dealing with Stress*, London: British Association of Social Workers/Macmillan.

Tite, R. (1993), 'How teachers define and respond to child abuse: the distinction between theoretical and reportable cases', *Child Abuse and Neglect*, **17**, 591–603.

United Nations (1989), *The Conventions on the Rights of the Child*, New York, NY: UNICEF.

Utting, W. (1991), *Children in the Public Care: A Review of Residential Child Care*, London: HMSO.

Utting, W. (1993), Foreword, in Evans, M. and Miller, C., *Partnership in Child Protection*, London: Office for Public Management/National Institute of Social Work.

Warner, N. (1993), *Choosing with Care*, London: HMSO.

Index

the **ABC** of
Child Protection

JEAN MOORE

"...an excellent source of information on the subject. If you buy this for your own reference shelf, you will take it down again and again to help you make sense of the child protection cases which all too often come your way." **The Magistrate**

The ABC of Child Protection examines four faces of abuse in detail: physical abuse, children caught up in marital violence, the much neglected subject of neglect, and sexual abuse.

The painful stresses experienced by the worker are not forgotten and emphasis is put upon the specific skills required in child protection work. There is a lively chapter on face-to-face work with abused children and the complexities of child protection conferences are helpfully analysed with particular reference to the attendance of parents and children.

The black perspective is given prominence with contributions from Emmanuel Okine and David Divine. A chapter by Caroline Ball describes the contents and implications of the 1989 Children Act. Issues relating to racism, sexism, classism, ageism and disabilityism are honestly tackled.

Jean Moore is a child abuse consultant and freelance trainer.

1992   224 pages   1 85742 027 6   £8.95

Price subject to change without notification

arena

The Police and Social Workers

Second Edition

Terry Thomas

Social workers and police officers are in daily contact with one another in various areas of their work. This book offers a clear guide to that inter-agency work and critically examines how it is carried out in practice.

This second edition of the book has been substantially revised to take account of changes in the law, policy and procedures affecting both police and social workers. In particular the Children Act 1989, The Criminal Justice Act 1991 and the findings of the Royal Commission on Criminal Justice 1993. The opportunity has also been taken to revise parts of the original text to ensure as clear a light as possible is thrown on police-social work collaboration – illustrating both the positive and the negative.

Terry Thomas is Senior Lecturer in Social Work at Leeds Metropolitan University.

1994   346 pages   1 85742 157 4   £14.95

Price subject to change without notification

arena

The Children Act *1989*:
Putting it into Practice
Mary Ryan

This book provides a practical guide to those parts of the Children Act 1989 that relate to the provision of services by local authorities to children and families; the powers and duties of local authorities in such circumstances; care and supervision proceedings; and child protection issues.

The book is a unique combination of information on the legal framework contained in the Act, regulations and guidance and information on good social work and legal practice, relevant research and recent case law. It is grounded on the author's practical experience of providing an advice and advocacy service for families; providing training for social workers, lawyers and other child care professionals; being involved with the development of the legislation from the consultation period in the early 1980s, through the parliamentary process, and the subsequent consultation on regulations, guidance and court rules.

Mary Ryan, the Co-Director of the Family Rights Group, is a solicitor who after working in private practice as a family lawyer, was the Family Rights Group's legal advisor for 10 years.

1994   256 pages

Hbk   1 85742 192 2   £30.00   Pbk   1 85742 193 0   £14.95

Price subject to change without notification

arena

THE essential SOCIAL WORKER

An introduction to professional practice in the 1990s

THIRD EDITION

MARTIN DAVIES

This third edition has been radically revised and updated and contains an entirely new chapter providing a clear outline of the historical and policy-related framework within which social work operates in areas of particular practice - child care, disability, mental health, old age and criminal justice.

The Essential Social Worker defends the idea of a broadly based profession seeking to maintain disadvantaged people in the community. It bravely confronts the shallowness of many short-term fashions and argues that social work is a uniquely humane contributor to the achievement of welfare in the 1990s and beyond.

A careful reading will ensure that the student gains an understanding of the role of social work in a complex urban society and develops an awareness of the debates which surround it. Social work is often subject to public criticism, but, as the author shows, it has continued to grow in scale and in influence throughout the 20th century, and, although its structure will continue to evolve, social work will remain essential in any society which regards itself as democratic and humane.

Martin Davies is Executive Director of the School of Social Work, University of East Anglia.

1994   240 pages   Hbk   1 85742 100 0   £29.95
Pbk   1 85742 101 9   £12.95

Price subject to change without notification

arena

LAW for
SOCIAL WORKERS:
An Introduction
2ND EDITION
Caroline Ball

The second edition of this book provides a basic introduction, for those with little knowledge of law and the legal system, to the legal context of social work with different client groups. The Children Act 1989 has come into force since publication of the first edition of this book, and the section on children and families reflects the radical changes which have resulted. An outline of the law relating to mental health, housing, education, the criminal process and young offenders similarly reflects the impact of the National Health Service and Community Care Act 1990 and the Criminal Justice Act 1991, on work with other client groups.

Probation officers and local authority social workers require a sound and basic competence in the application of law at the time of qualification, which needs reinforcing and updating throughout professional practice. This book will aid both the acquisition and the development of the knowledge base necessary for competence.

Caroline Ball is Lecturer in Law at the School of Social Work, University of East Anglia.

1992   140 pages   1 85742 067 5   £8.95

Price subject to change without notification

arena